THE 50 MOST IMPORTANT
TEACHINGS *of* THE BIBLE

JIM GEORGE

HARVEST HOUSE PUBLISHERS
EUGENE, OREGON

Cover by Dugan Design Group, Bloomington, Minnesota

THE 50 MOST IMPORTANT TEACHINGS OF THE BIBLE
Copyright © 2015 Jim George
Published by Harvest House Publishers
Eugene, Oregon 97402
www.harvesthousepublishers.com

ISBN 978-0-7369-6017-5 (pbk.)
ISBN 978-0-7369-6019-9 (eBook)

Printed in the United States of America

15 16 17 18 19 20 21 22 23 / BP-CD / 10 9 8 7 6 5 4 3 2 1

Contents

Before You Begin 5

1. The Bible Is a Totally Unique Book 7
2. The Universe Didn't Just Come into Existence
   by Chance 11
3. God Is Both Three…and One 17
4. Jesus Was a Man, but Much More Than a Man 23
5. Every Person Is Created in God's Image 27
6. The Bible Is the Ultimate Handbook for Life 31
7. The Holy Spirit Lives Inside Every Believer 35
8. Jesus Is Alive and Well on Planet Earth 39
9. In Jesus, All Is Forgiven 43
10. You Are Worth More Than You Think 47
11. Caring for Those in Need Is One of God's
    Top Priorities 51
12. We Should Forgive Just as We Are Forgiven 55
13. Prayer Is a Way You Can Connect with God 59
14. You Are Made to Live Forever 65
15. Satan Is Not as Powerful as You Think He Is 69
16. Ignore Satan at Your Own Risk 73
17. Christians Are Perfect, and They Will Be! 77
18. It's Not About What You Do, but About What
    Christ Did 83
19. Even When It May Not Seem Like It,
    God Really Is in Control 87
20. You Cannot Escape from God's Presence 91
21. Nothing Can Separate You from God's Love 95
22. Sin Has Consequences, Both Now and Eternally . . . 99
23. God Has a Wonderful Purpose for Your Life 105

24. In the Spiritual Life, No Pain, No Gain 111

25. Give Yourself Grace…Because God Does 115

26. This World Is Not Your Home 119

27. God Is Real and He Is Not Silent 123

28. Sin Is Not Just an Action, but a Nature 127

29. It's Really All About Love 131

30. Jesus Really Is Coming Back 135

31. Jesus Prays for You and Me 139

32. When Jesus Died, So Did Death 143

33. One Birth Is Not Enough 147

34. Rescue Is Only Part of the Story 153

35. The Holy Spirit Is the Secret Weapon
of Every Christian 157

36. What Is God Like? Look at Jesus 161

37. God Wants to Be Intimate with You 165

38. The Lord Is My Shepherd 169

39. Turn or Burn 173

40. How Much Water Is Enough? 179

41. Membership Has Its Privileges 185

42. Jesus Brings a Different Kind of Happiness 191

43. Angels Are Not Just Something You Put on the
Top of Your Christmas Tree 197

44. When God Makes a Promise, He Keeps It 203

45. Jesus Walks with You, and When Necessary,
Carries You 207

46. This News Is So Good, Don't Keep It to Yourself! . . . 211

47. You Ain't Seen Nothing Yet! 215

48. Nothing Takes God by Surprise 221

49. Heavenly Living Starts Here and Now. 225

50. In the End, God Wins! 229

Before You Begin

It's been said that what you believe is how you behave. That is, what you believe about God, His written revelation, the Bible, and His ultimate revelation, His Son, will define how you live your life. My goal for this book about what the Bible teaches is to help give you a better understanding of the key teachings that are critical for your growth as a Christian. While all of the teachings in the Bible are important because they all communicate what God wants us to know about Him, there are some teachings that are more foundational than others. The question, of course, is this: Where do you start?

I have written *The 50 Most Important Teachings in the Bible* to help provide you with a "starting point." These 50 teachings will guide your initial study of major themes such as...

> God as the Creator of the universe and His dealings with man
>
> Jesus' relationship with the Father and the Holy Spirit
>
> The nature of the Bible as the written revelation of God
>
> God's solution to the problem of sin
>
> The ministry of Jesus and the Holy Spirit
>
> God's plans for the future, including the end of time

As you read along, keep in mind that the teachings presented in this book are not ranked in any particular order. And because the intent of this book is to provide the basic essentials, if you would like to dig deeper, then you'll want to seek other sources for additional information on a given topic.

It is my prayer that this volume, along with your personal reading and study of the Bible, will assist you in fulfilling God's desire that you "grow in the grace and knowledge of our Lord and Savior Jesus Christ. To him be glory both now and forever! Amen" (2 Peter 3:18).

Jim George

1

The Bible Is a Totally Unique Book

*The grass withers and the flowers fall, but
the word of our God endures forever
(Isaiah 40:8).*

*All Scripture is God-breathed and is useful for teaching,
rebuking, correcting and training in righteousness
(2 Timothy 3:16).*

*The word of God is alive and powerful. It is sharper
than the sharpest two-edged sword, cutting between
soul and spirit, between joint and marrow. It
exposes our innermost thoughts and desires
(Hebrews 4:12 NLT).*

Several years ago my wife and I traveled to France. Instead of finding a hotel in Paris, we decided to stay outside of the city in a small country village so we could wind down after working hard to meet several book deadlines. I lasted about two days in the quiet village before I was ready for a road trip (or in our case, a train trip) into Paris. Our first stop, as you might guess, was a ride up to the top of the Eiffel Tower. Then we were off to the Louvre, one of the world's premiere museums of art. And even though I'm not an educated lover of art, my first thought was to locate the *Mona Lisa*, which is one of the most famous paintings of all time, painted by the famous Italian artist Leonardo da Vinci from about 1504 to 1519.

Even though the *Mona Lisa* is special, it pales in comparison to the uniqueness of the Bible! There are many masterpieces in the art world, but there is only one Bible. The Bible is unlike any other book because it was written by God. It is also the most widely read book in the world, having been translated into hundreds of languages. Consider these reasons why the Bible is unique:

The Bible is a book of many books. When you skim the pages of a Bible, what do you notice? As the pages fly by, you'll see right away that the Bible contains many different books made up of varying numbers of chapters. The 66 books of the Bible were written by more than 40 authors, who originally wrote it in Hebrew, Greek, and Aramaic. Their writing of this volume took place over the course of some 2000 years.

No other book can boast of this unique composition, and the most amazing thing about these 66 books by 40-plus authors is their one unified message describing and pointing toward Jesus Christ. The message that God, the Creator of the universe, wanted mankind to understand was the relationship He had with Jesus, and how that relationship affects all mankind both now and on into eternity.

The Bible is the written Word of God. Starting in the Old Testament, the authors of the Bible asserted more than 3800 times that what they were writing is the Word of God. In addition, the phrases "the word of God" or the "oracles of God" occur more than 40 times in the New Testament.

How could this be possible? How could the words that make up the Bible come from the hearts and minds of men, and at the same time, from the heart and mind of God? The apostle Peter explained it this way: "Prophecy never had its origin in the human will, but prophets, though human, spoke from God as they were carried along by the Holy Spirit" (2 Peter 1:21).

The phrase "carried along" means that even though the human authors were the ones who were writing Scripture, God, the Holy Spirit, "managed" them as they wrote. It would be like a manager in a store or in a corporate department at work. He or she doesn't do the work, they just oversee and direct others toward finishing the work. In the same way, the writers of Scripture used their own vocabulary, personalities, and thought processes, to compose and record what God wanted written. God, the Holy Spirit, was watching over the authors of the 66 books of the Bible and managing them toward a final product whose content was made up of the exact words God intended, and without error. It couldn't be any other way because God, "who does not lie" (Titus 1:2), produced a book that was without error in the original.

The Bible is indestructible. No other book in all of history has survived as many attempts to destroy it. The Old and New Testaments have stood the test of time, with some of the texts dating back to 3000 years ago. Even though the original manuscripts of each of the books of the Bible have been lost, thousands of copies have been produced down through the centuries and have survived. With the thousands of early copies of all or parts of the Bible, scholars believe they have reclaimed close to 99.9 percent of the original text that was without error. Note God's promise concerning His Word in Isaiah 40:8: "The grass withers and the flowers fall, but the word of our God endures forever."

What Does This Mean for You?

As you can gather from my story about viewing the *Mona Lisa*, I made quite an effort and paid a significant price to see this well-known painting. It took a day to fly to Europe, and another day to travel by train to get to Paris, but now I can say, "I've seen the *Mona Lisa!*"

Then I have to ask myself, "So what?" My life hasn't changed as a result of viewing that work of art. I cannot say I'm a better person as a result of that visit. In fact, there's a sense in which I'm now worse off because of the expense of making that trip!

But what about the Bible? History and God Himself have attested that the Bible is the greatest and most unique book ever written. Its message is of greatest importance and can change a life. You can read it, memorize its truths, and learn something new every time you open it. By contrast, the *Mona Lisa* resides behind a glass and can only be admired from a distance of about 20 feet. And it has no power to bring about change in your life.

So it makes sense that the Bible is the most popular book ever written. After all, it is God's personal message to mankind—and to you. In it, He offers you words of encouragement, direction for your life, and wisdom for daily living and decision making. Most important of all, He lets you know how you can experience eternal life with Him!

Because all that is true about the Bible, don't you think you should spend some time—or more time—reading it? When you do, you will continue to discover all that this amazing book has to offer. *And* your life will be changed!

"I believe the Bible is the best gift God has ever given
to man. All the good from the Savior of the world
is communicated to us through this book."

ABRAHAM LINCOLN
16th President of the United States

2

The Universe Didn't Just Come into Existence by Chance

In the beginning you laid the foundations of the earth, and the heavens are the work of your hands (Psalm 102:25).

The heavens are yours, and yours also the earth; you founded the world and all that is in it (Psalm 89:11).

By the word of the LORD the heavens were made, their starry host by the breath of his mouth (Psalm 33:6).

Have you ever met anyone who wanted to relive their high school years? Well, I certainly haven't! Maybe that's because when I was in high school, I had no idea where life would eventually take me. But as I look back now, one thing I do know is that where I am today didn't just happen by chance. Take, for instance, how I became a pharmacist. A local pharmacist in the small town where I grew up attended my church. One Sunday he asked me if I would like a job working in his pharmacy.

He said he had observed my conduct and watched my involvement with the youth group at church, and thought I would be a hard worker and would interact well with the customers.

Was this a chance action on his part? No, not at all. It was by design. This man made a decision to offer me a job based on his observations of me and my character. This was a case of cause-and-effect. Chance had nothing to do with my ultimately becoming a pharmacist.

Think about it—very few things in life, if any, happen by chance. Have you ever thought about how life began? If you are a Christian, you accept what the Bible says about the origin of life: "In the beginning God created the heavens and the earth" (Genesis 1:1). From the very first verse in the Bible to the last book, Revelation, we see repeated declarations that God created the universe and everything in it. "You are worthy, our Lord and God…for you created all things" (Revelation 4:11).

How did the world come into existence? People through the ages have offered many different explanations, but Christians believe that God created the universe.

So what are the options for those who don't believe God made the Earth? What explanations are there for those who cannot or will not believe the biblical account of creation? The primary response from those who say creation didn't come about by design is that it happened through evolution—by chance.

Those who hold to evolution claim their view is supported by science. But ultimately, they still have to say that everything we see around us somehow came about by chance, by random processes that occurred without the help of any outside forces. And how did it all get started? There are many points at which the theory of evolution cannot be backed by science because certain things cannot be verified or tested. So people fall back on different explanations about what might have happened, such as the Big Bang theory, which speculates that our expanding universe goes back to a single originating point of some sort.

While there are elements of the theory of evolution which cannot be tested scientifically, there are also elements of creation that are supported by scientific evidence. To explore this more is beyond the scope of this book, and there are many good books available that explain how the Bible and science both affirm our universe was created by a Designer.

Whatever your view, when you consider the vast expanses of all that exists around us, we cannot help but consider the following:

The world around us teaches you how finite you really are. The scope of our universe exceeds the grasp of the human mind. Modern astronomers, through research done with satellites and the Hubble telescope, have estimated there are 100 billion solar systems, each one of them like ours—having its own sun and billions of stars. You may not be able to explain the universe, but you have to admit that its scope is beyond your ability to fully understand. That should make you wonder: Did this all come about by random chance, or by intelligent design? A universe of this magnitude and complexity had to have some greater force that brought it into existence.

So why not accept the Bible's account that the most powerful force—God!—created those 100 billion solar systems? It seems unreasonable for us, as finite beings, not to look to the infinite for answers for how we got here and what our purpose is. Don't let your finite mind try to overrule the infinite. "The fool has said in his heart, 'There is no God'" (Psalm 14:1).

The world around us points to God's existence and your responsibility. Does anyone have an excuse for not believing in God? The Bible says no. God has revealed Himself through creation. "The heavens declare the glory of God; the skies proclaim the work of his hands" (Psalm 19:1). As Creator, God assumes a place of preeminence. "The God who made the world and everything in it is the Lord of heaven and earth" (Acts 17:24). Every person as a created being must either accept or reject God's place of authority and man's responsibility to God. There is no middle ground, no place for a wait-and-see mentality. The day is coming when God will judge every person's response to Him. At that point there will be no excuse for rejecting God (Revelation 20:13).

Do this. The next time there is a clear night sky in your area, find a dark place outdoors and look up. Look for the infinite God in His infinite creation, and hear His call: "The heavens declare the glory of God; the skies proclaim the work of his hands" (Psalm 19:1).

The world around us teaches about your relationship to God. The Bible declares that God is the Creator, and as such is distinct from you, His creation. God is eternal and in control of the universe. Yet out of the millions of stars and the great expanse of the heavens, He chose to focus His creative efforts on making man in His own image. God said, "Let us make mankind in our image, in our likeness" (Genesis 1:26).

Can you believe it? As the great Creator of all things, God set apart mankind—that includes you—as special in His eyes. Just as a father loves his children, God loves you and wants what is best for you. By contrast, chance cannot offer you this kind of personal relationship. Chance can only offer you a purposeless, impersonal existence in this life and an eternity without hope.

The world around us teaches about the worth of man. The fact you and all mankind are created by God, not as mere animals but in God's image, should tell you something about your worth. Human worth is not based on possessions, achievements, physical characteristics, or nationality. Instead, it's based on being made in God's image. Those who can't or won't believe in creation also reject the God of creation. As a result, they view their fellow man as just another evolved creature with no special worth. But knowing that you bear God's image should cause you to ask the question, How should I properly relate to God, whose image I bear, and to my fellow man, who also bears God's image? Jesus was asked a similar question and this is the answer He gave: "'Love the Lord your God with all your heart and with all your soul and with all your mind.' This is the first and greatest commandment. And the second is like it: 'Love your neighbor as yourself'" (Matthew 22:37-39).

What Does This Mean for You?

God, your Creator, wants the best for you and has authored a book, the Bible, to guide you through life. The Bible contains everything you need to know about how you can have a relationship with God, and how that relationship moves you from being merely a creation to being a beloved son or daughter to God.

The question every person needs to answer is this: Why not choose the biblical option of creation by God rather than by chance? It has so much more to offer you! Moses admonished the people of his day to make a choice: "This day I call the heavens and the earth as witnesses against you that I have set before you life and death, blessings and curses. Now choose life" (Deuteronomy 30:19).

3

God Is Both Three…and One

*You were shown these things so that you might know
that the LORD is God; besides him there is no other
(Deuteronomy 4:35).*

*As soon as Jesus was baptized, he went up out of the
water. At that moment heaven was opened, and he
saw the Spirit of God descending like a dove and
alighting on him. And a voice from heaven said, "This
is my Son, whom I love; with him I am well pleased"
(Matthew 3:16-17).*

*Go and make disciples of all nations, baptizing them in the
name of the Father and of the Son and of the Holy Spirit
(Matthew 28:19).*

Is there anything you don't know? All you have to do is look at
your old report cards, right? Or play a game of Scrabble or Trivial Pursuit. The answer is painfully clear: Of course you don't know
everything. There are always new things to learn.

But just because we don't know or understand something
doesn't mean we cannot benefit from it. For example, I don't have
a clue as to how my computer works. But that doesn't keep me
from using it. The same principle is true when it comes to certain

truths in God's Word. Just because you or I don't understand something affirmed by Scripture doesn't mean we cannot benefit from it.

One good example of this is the Trinity, or the truth that God is three-in-one. Our finite minds have a difficult time grasping this truth, but that doesn't mean we should ignore it. For some people, the truth of the Godhead is a problem, to the point they deny it simply because the word *Trinity* isn't in the Bible. But if we read Scripture carefully, we can definitely see affirmation of the fact there is only one God who is of three eternal Persons who are the same in substance or essence, but distinct in their roles as follows:

> God exists as the *invisible Father*, from whom all revelation proceeds and who sent…
>
> *the Son*, who mediates between God and man, and historically manifested that revelation as a human, God in flesh, and
>
> *the Holy Spirit*, who was sent by the Father and, as God, divinely applies the revelation of God to men.

Tertullian, a third-century theologian, was the first to coin the term *Trinity*. He stated that the Trinity was divinely revealed because, from a human standpoint, it seems so absurd that no one could have invented it!

God's name itself implies plurality. The Bible states in no uncertain terms that there is but one God. "Hear, O Israel: The LORD our God, the LORD is one" (Deuteronomy 6:4). But throughout the Old Testament, the Hebrew name for God—"Elohim"—is in the plural, indicating more than one. Genesis, the first book of the Bible, make three references to God with the pronoun *us*: God said, "Let us make man" (1:26); "the LORD God said, 'Behold, the man has become like one of us, knowing good and evil'" (3:22); and "Come, let us go down and there confuse their language" (11:7).

What does the Bible say about each member of the Trinity?

The Father is God. As the Creator of the universe and of man, God is often spoken of as the Father. Just as a human father has a special relationship with his children, so too God as Creator also has a special relationship with His creation. Jesus said when you pray, you should begin your prayers with, "Our Father in heaven" (Matthew 6:9). Here are a few of the Father's characteristics:

> Omniscient—He has infinite awareness, understanding, and insight.

> Omnipotent—He has unlimited authority, power, and influence.

> Omnipresent—He is present in all places at all times.

> Immutable—He is not capable of or susceptible to change. He has been and will always be the same.

> Eternal—He is infinite. He has no beginning and will have no end.

Next, let's look at some facts about Jesus and the Holy Spirit and their attributes. You will notice they possess the same attributes as God the Father.

Jesus is co-equal with God the Father. The apostle Paul is considered to be the architect of orthodox theology. He made the fact of Jesus being co-equal to God very clear when he wrote that "we wait for the blessed hope—the appearing of the glory of our great God and Savior, Jesus Christ" (Titus 2:13). Other passages in the Bible also speak of Jesus as God and ascribe God's attributes to Jesus:

> —Jesus showed omniscience—"Knowing their thoughts, Jesus said..." (Matthew 9:4).

> —Jesus showed omnipresence—He said, "I am with you always, to the very end of the age" (Matthew 28:20).

> —Jesus showed eternality—"In the beginning was the Word, and the Word was with God, and the Word was God...The Word became flesh and made His dwelling among us" (John 1:1,14).

—Jesus was ascribed holiness—Peter wrote, "We have come to believe and to know that you are the Holy One of God" (John 6:69).

—Jesus was ascribed the works of God—We see in Scripture that Jesus was involved in creation (John 1:3), He is a sovereign ruler (Matthew 25:31), and He sustains the universe (Colossians 1:17).

—Jesus is worthy of worship and honor—Note what Thomas declared about Jesus—he called Him "my Lord and my God" (John 20:28).

—Jesus' name is associated equally with that of God the Father—"In the name of the Father and of the Son…" (Matthew 28:19).

What other conclusion can we come to, other than that Jesus is God and is co-equal with Him?

The Holy Spirit is co-equal with God the Father and God the Son— He too is a person, and not a force, as some people mistakenly assume. Writers of both the Old and New Testaments help us understand the nature of the Holy Spirit:

The Holy Spirit is directly connected to God—In Acts 5:3-4, the apostle Peter told Ananias, "You have lied to the Holy Spirit… You have not lied just to human beings but to God."

The Holy Spirit's names speak of divinity—For example, Scripture speaks of the Holy Spirit as the "Spirit of God" (1 Corinthians 6:11), "Spirit of Christ" (Romans 8:9), and "Spirit of truth" (John 14:17).

The Holy Spirit possesses these (as well as all the other) divine attributes of God:

—Omniscience: "The Spirit searches all things, even the deep things of God…no one knows the thoughts of God except the Spirit of God" (1 Corinthians 2:10-11).

—Omnipresence: "Where can I go from your Spirit? Where can I flee from your presence?" (Psalm 139:7).

—Omnipotence: "The Spirit of God was hovering over the waters" (Genesis 1:2). He was "hovering" in the sense of participating in and protecting the work of creation.

What Does This Mean for You?

The Trinity is an important concept even though you may never fully understand it. Here's how the Trinity relates to your life: God who is spirit and cannot die, sent His Son to be born into the world as a physical human. His Son lived a perfect life, and the fact He was without sin qualified Him to be the perfect sacrifice necessary to pay for our sin. Three days after Jesus died on the cross, He rose from the dead, making salvation possible for all who believe in Him for eternal life. At the moment of salvation, the Spirit of God and of Jesus is sent to indwell us. The Holy Spirit's ministry is to lead, guide, protect, and equip us to live godly lives in an ungodly world.

If you are a Christian, the teaching of the Trinity is a key element of your faith. By keeping in mind the work each member of the Trinity does, you can direct petitions and prayers of thanks and worship to them. Furthermore, the perfect love and unity within the Godhead models for you the oneness and affection that should characterize your relationship with other believers within the body of Christ.

4

Jesus Was a Man, but Much More Than a Man

In the beginning was the Word, and the Word was with God, and the Word was God. He was with God in the beginning... The Word became flesh and made his dwelling among us... who came from the Father, full of grace and truth (John 1:1–2,14).

The angel said to her, "Do not be afraid, Mary; you have found favor with God. You will conceive and give birth to a son, and you are to call him Jesus. He will be great and will be called the Son of the Most High... The Holy Spirit will come on you, and the power of the Most High will overshadow you. So the holy one to be born will be called the Son of God" (Luke 1:30–32,35).

Have the same mindset as Christ Jesus: Who, being in very nature God, did not consider equality with God something to be used to his own advantage; rather, he made himself nothing by taking the very nature of a servant, being made in human likeness...being found in appearance as a man (Philippians 2:5–8).

Who is the greatest single figure that the world has ever produced? The Jews would say Abraham or Moses. Muslims would say Mohammed. Buddhists would say Buddha. The Chinese might say Confucius. But without a doubt, the greatest person who has ever lived was Jesus. That's remarkable when you consider He didn't write a book during His time on Earth. He never traveled more than a relatively short distance from His birthplace. He never had more than a few followers during His ministry. Yet very few people in the literate world have never heard the name *Jesus*. There are some who use the name as a curse word or a slang term or in derision, but nevertheless, His name is spoken and recognized by multitudes worldwide.

Why is that so? What sets Him apart from any other person in all history?

The Bible tells us Jesus was more than a man—much more. Let's see what it says:

Jesus existed prior to coming to Earth. God has no beginning and no end. He has always existed; otherwise, He could not be God. The Bible repeatedly and without explanation states that Jesus is God. Therefore, He had to have existed prior to coming to Earth. At the beginning of the Gospel of John, we read this: "In the beginning was the Word, and the Word was with God, and the Word was God. He was with God in the beginning" (John 1:1). When John spoke of "the Word," he was speaking of Jesus, the eternal Son of God who existed with God the Father before time began. Then John made this astounding statement: "The Word became flesh and made his dwelling among us" (verse 14).

God became a man! Jesus took upon Himself full humanity and lived as a man, but at the same time, He never ceased to be the eternal God who has always existed, the Creator and Sustainer of all things, the source of eternal life. After penning this amazing declaration, John spent the remainder of the book of John encouraging his readers to have faith not in an ordinary man, but in Jesus Christ—in God, who became a man (John 20:30-31).

Jesus is both human and divine. "The Word became flesh" means that God became human. In doing so, He became...

The perfect man—Jesus always said and did the right thing. This may be why evil men reacted so violently to His life, His ministry, and His message. They were enemies of God and killed the man whose perfection was a constant reminder of their unwillingness to repent of their sins.

The perfect teacher—Jesus' words are forever true and correct. In His teachings you are made aware of what is important to God's heart.

The perfect example—Jesus, who "came from the Father, [was] full of grace and truth" (John 1:14). He is a model of how you are to live. He took on "the very nature of a servant" (Philippians 2:8). How does God want you to live? Look to Jesus!

The perfect sacrifice—Because Jesus was perfect, He could die as the perfect sacrifice for all sin. God is holy and cannot accept sin in His presence. Only a perfect sacrifice would be acceptable for cleansing us of sin. Jesus' death fully satisfied the Father's requirement that sin be punished.

Jesus is the Savior of the world. Joseph, who was betrothed to Mary, had a dream in which he was told by an angel to follow through on his plan to wed Mary, for her child would be special. The angel said, "You are to give him the name Jesus, because he will save his people from their sins" (Matthew 1:21). The name "Jesus" means "the Lord saves." Jesus came to Earth to save us from our sins. There is nothing we can do to save ourselves—only Jesus can rescue us from the power and penalty of sin.

Jesus not only created the world, He also became the Savior of the world. You might want to pause right now and worship Him by offering up a prayer of praise and thanksgiving to Jesus for His willingness to die on the cross to pay the penalty for your sins. Then ask Him to strengthen you and and help you gain victory over the power of the daily "sin that so easily entangles" (Hebrews 12:1).

What Does This Mean for You?

Jesus expects you to live for Him. The Christian faith isn't about dying—it's about living. If Jesus is your Savior, you are no longer alone, for He now lives in you. He is your power for living and your hope for the future. His Spirit living in you empowers you moment by moment to follow in Jesus' footsteps. Jesus told His disciples that if they loved Him, they would keep His commandments. Living for Jesus means you willingly choose to follow His commands.

Where do you find those commands? Read through the Gospels on a regular basis. Read what Jesus said about living for God. Read about how Jesus responded to the pressures of daily life. In His Word, the Bible, Jesus has provided help for you to live the Christian life. It will guide you like a lamp shining in the darkest of nights. He has also given spiritually gifted men to the church who help give wise counsel and direction.

Living for Jesus requires a willful effort on your part. The resources are available to you. Are you ready for the challenge?

5

Every Person Is Created in God's Image

*God said, "Let us make mankind in our image, in
our likeness…" So God created mankind in
his own image, in the image of God he created
them; male and female he created them
(Genesis 1:26–27).*

*Just as we have borne the image of the earthly man, so
shall we bear the image of the heavenly man
(1 Corinthians 15:49).*

*We all, who with unveiled faces contemplate
the Lord's glory, are being transformed into
his image with ever-increasing glory…
(2 Corinthians 3:18).*

Recently I was in downtown Honolulu for a dental appointment, and on my return home, I made a wrong turn. As a result I ended up on a road that took me past the Ali'io-lani Hale, the home of the Supreme Court of Hawaii, as well as an impressive statue of Kamehameha the Great, the king who united the Hawaiian Islands.

Thomas Gould, a Boston sculptor, was commissioned to create the statue. Even though photographs of Polynesians were sent to

Gould for reference purposes, evidently he ignored them. Kamehameha looks more like a European, and even has a Roman nose. This may be due to the fact that Gould was living in Italy at the time he made the sculpture. While the statue is impressive, unfortunately, it doesn't accurately represent Kamehameha.

As we come to the Bible's teaching that every person is created in God's image, you may be wondering, *What exactly does it mean that we are made in God's image?* As we consider the answer, we learn some important truths about the significance that God is our Creator.

Accepting the fact God is our Creator is a basic step of faith. The first words of any book are extremely important, for they set the theme for the book. When the Bible opens by saying, "In the beginning God created the heavens and the earth" (Genesis 1:1), that lets us know immediately that God, as Creator, is a key focal point of everything that follows. Later, the Bible says, "By faith we understand that the universe was formed at God's command, so that what is seen was not made out of what was visible" (Hebrews 11:3). As a worshipper of your Creator, you also become subject to His power, authority, wisdom, and direction. His image in you demands that you reflect that image.

God's image does not refer to physical qualities. God did not create us exactly like Himself—for example, God has no physical body. Instead, we are a reflection of His character. Like God, we have the ability to communicate, to reason, to love, to have patience, to be faithful, and to forgive others. Obviously we will never be totally like God because He is God—the Supreme Being—and we are not. But when we live as He desires for us to live, we reflect His character to a watching world.

God's image in us means we belong to Him. On one occasion when Jesus was confronted by a group of Jewish religious leaders, they tried to trap Him with a trick question: "Is it right to pay the imperial tax to Caesar or not?" (Mark 12:14). What did Jesus do? He had them bring Him a Roman coin with Caesar's image on it. He then gave this well-known answer: "Give back to Caesar what is Caesar's and to God what is God's" (verse 17). Jesus said the coin bearing the emperor's image should be given to the emperor. But a life that bears the image of God belongs to God. Jesus defined what it means to belong to God when He said, "Love the Lord your God with all your heart and with all your soul and with all your strength and with all your mind" (Luke 10:27).

Are you giving God all that is rightfully His? Give God your heart and life—you bear His image!

God's image is the basis for human self-worth. Actually, it is better to say "God-worth." Because you were created by God and you bear His image, you are important to Him. You have "God-worth."

When you are criticized by others or you get down on yourself, remember that God has made you in His image—He has given you life, as well as the abilities you have. The psalmist expressed it this way: "I praise you because I am fearfully and wonderfully made; your works are wonderful, I know that full well" (Psalm 139:14).

Knowing you are a person of worth in God's eyes should prompt you to praise God as the psalmist did. And knowing God loves you should excite you to want to be a positive spiritual influence on others.

God's image is important in human relationships. Because all humans are created in God's image, all of them possess certain qualities that distinguish them from animals. This "image" gives man morality, reason, creativity, and worth. When we interact with other people, we are interacting with other beings made by God—beings to whom God offers the gift of eternal life. Under ideal circumstances, this common characteristic should enhance our relationships. Unfortunately, sin makes it impossible for us to have perfect, problem-free relationships. Only Jesus Christ can restore broken relationships, especially your relationship with God. Thankfully, "he has reconciled you by Christ's physical body through death to present you holy in his sight, without blemish and free from accusation" (Colossians 1:22).

God's image in us is marred by sin. When God created man in His image, life was pure and unhindered in the Garden of Eden. God and man had a perfect relationship. There was perfect love between God and man and between man and woman. All the qualities inherent in the concept of God's image were present.

But with mankind's fall into sin, God's image in man became distorted—it became warped and twisted. The farther away man moved from God in his sinful behavior, the dimmer that image appeared. Jesus' payment for sin on the cross made it possible for a broken relationship with God to be restored: "God made him who had no sin to be sin for us, so that in him we might become the righteousness of God" (2 Corinthians 5:21).

God restores man's original image in Christ. God created a perfect world, and He created man perfect in His own image. For reasons we cannot understand, God allowed sin to both mar His creation and distort His image in man. But all through the Bible we see that God has always had a plan to restore and "upgrade" man's likeness to God. The apostle Paul states it this way: "Those God foreknew he also predestined to be conformed to the image of his Son" (Romans 8:29).

God's plan is to make those who are His own into the image of His Son, Jesus Christ. So, as it was at creation, God's people will once again possess the image of God in all its glory!

What Does This Mean for You?

Being made in God's image is a great privilege. Of all God's creation, only mankind was created in His image. Because you bear God's image, He has a claim on your life. Rejoice in your relationship with God. Embrace your likeness to Him. And purpose to learn more about your Creator. Begin today by taking time to worship Him, and commit yourself to gladly living in a way that reflects His image.

6

The Bible Is the Ultimate Handbook for Life

*Your word is a lamp for my feet, a light on my path
(Psalm 119:105).*

*All Scripture... is useful for teaching, rebuking, correcting
and training in righteousness, so that the servant of
God may be thoroughly equipped for every good work
(2 Timothy 3:16–17).*

*His divine power has given us everything
we need for a godly life
(2 Peter 1:3).*

Getting a new job is an exciting adventure. But then comes that moment when your boss drops a ten-pound book in your lap and says, "This is the company policies handbook. Everything you will ever need to know about this company's operating procedures is in this book. You'll also find important information about your responsibilities to the company. You might want to become familiar with this handbook."

What exactly is a handbook? One helpful definition is that it's "a concise manual or reference book providing specific information or instruction about a subject or place." If you think about it, that's what the Bible does too. It is a concise reference and instruction book for living a life that is pleasing to God. For that reason, as your boss said about the company handbook, "You might want to become familiar with it."

Yes, the Bible is a handbook. Let's learn more about how it can help us:

The Bible introduces you to God's standard for living. Very early in the writing of the Bible, God gave Moses a set of rules for the people of Israel to live by. These were the Ten Commandments (Exodus 20:3-17). The first four addressed how the people were to honor and worship God. The last six spoke of how the people were to interact with others. In the New Testament, Jesus clarified God's standard when He said, "Be perfect, therefore, as your Father in heaven is perfect" (Matthew 5:48).

With these words, Jesus set an unattainable standard for us to live by. His words summed up what the Ten Commandments demanded. As you can see, this standard is impossible to meet. Yet God could not lower it without compromising His own perfection. God, who is perfect, could not set an imperfect standard of righteousness. The amazing truth of the gospel is that Christ met this standard on your behalf (1 Corinthians 5:21).

The Bible is a guide. What is the purpose of a guide? To help you find your way. Do you have any idea where you are going? Well, God stands ready to point you in the right direction, and He has given you a guidebook in the Bible. "This God is our God for ever and ever; he will be our guide even to the end" (Psalm 48:14).

Do you have decisions to make? Then you can seek direction from God in His handbook, the Bible. Is there any area of life and living where the Bible cannot help? No—"his divine power has given us everything we need for a godly life" (2 Peter 1:3). Everything! The Bible has to be the best handbook ever if it can make this kind of claim!

The Bible is a light. As Psalm 119:105 says, "Your word is a lamp for my feet, a light on my path." Whereas a guide leads you on unknown paths, a lamp provides the light for the path you are on so you don't trip, fall, or get lost. In this life, you will have times when you walk "through the valley of shadow of death" (Psalm 23:4 NASB). But the Bible can be your light to show you the way ahead so you won't stumble. It will help you to discern truth from error and expose Satan with all his lies and deception. Study the Bible so you will be able to see your way clearly and stay on the right path—God's path. Let it be your guidebook for life.

The Bible is a map. A guide leads the way, a lamp lights the way, but a map shows the way. Do you realize that Earth is not your home, that you are only passing through? The apostle Peter calls us "foreigners and exiles" in 1 Peter 2:11. As a pilgrim in this world, you must study God's map to know the way. If you ignore the map, you will wander aimlessly through life and risk missing out on all God has for you while you are here on Earth. Life is a difficult journey with unpredictable twists and turns. To ensure you don't lose your way, look to your Bible. It is your road map, indicating safe routes and obstacles to avoid. It will point you to your final destination—heaven.

The Bible equips you. Most handbooks are training manuals. If you want to do your job well, then you must read and follow the instructions in the manual. It's the same way with the Bible. Second Timothy 3:16 says the Bible is useful or "profitable" (NASB). There are not many things in life that you can say are absolutely 100 percent profitable, but the Bible makes this claim for itself. It is profitable for...

> Teaching—The Bible is "God-breathed"—it's from God Himself, which makes its teachings a source of authority on how you should live your life.

> Reproof—The Bible offers rebuke to those in sin. Who better to hold you accountable for right living than God Himself through His Word!

Correction—The Bible explains what it means to turn away from sin and toward righteous living.

Training or instruction—The Bible shows you how to live a life that pleases God and glorifies His name.

The Bible gives wisdom. Where does wisdom come from? God is the source of all wisdom. And because God is the author of the Bible you can be assured that it is filled with His wisdom. But wisdom doesn't just happen. You have to decide to "get wisdom" (Proverbs 4:5). This requires reading and studying the truths of the Bible. Wisdom is then produced as you apply God's life-changing truths to your life.

As you follow the Bible, you'll make fewer mistakes. Be wise! Read your Bible, discover its truths, and apply its wisdom moment by moment as you live out each day. Pray Moses' prayer: "Teach us to number our days, that we may gain a heart of wisdom" (Psalm 90:12).

What Does This Mean for You?

You can count on the Bible 100 percent of the time for 100 percent perfect instruction and information. It is indeed the 100 percent perfect handbook for life—which makes it an essential resource. Remember, the Bible shows you the way to eternal life, and is given to you "so that [you] may be thoroughly equipped for every good work" (2 Timothy 3:17). Be faithful to study God's Word so you will know how to do God's work and endure the challenges you face.

7

The Holy Spirit Lives
Inside Every Believer

*I will ask the Father, and he will give you another
advocate to help you and be with you forever—the
Spirit of truth. The world cannot accept him, because
it neither sees him nor knows him. But you know
him, for he lives with you and will be in you
(John 14:16-17).*

*John baptized with water, but in a few days
you will be baptized with the Holy Spirit
(Acts 1:5).*

*All of them were filled with the Holy Spirit and began
to speak in other tongues as the Spirit enabled them
(Acts 2:4).*

Often Christianity is described as one of the great world religions. If by *religion* people mean a specific set of beliefs and
practices generally agreed upon by a number of persons or sects,
they are correct. But Christianity is more than a religion. It is a
relationship with God—an intimate personal relationship with the
Lord Jesus Christ.

How is a relationship with God possible? Through the work
of the Holy Spirit, who indwells all believers and is therefore

personally involved and active in the life of each believer. No other religion can make quite the same claim. Only Christians can say that their God—the one true God—actually lives in them. How can this be? Let's see what the Bible says.

The Holy Spirit is God. The Bible states in no uncertain terms that there is but one God: "Hear, O Israel: The LORD our God, the LORD is one" (Deuteronomy 6:4). Yet the Bible speaks of the Holy Spirit as a person who has the attributes of God—He was part of creation (Psalm 104:30), He knows all truth (John 14:16), and He is omnipresent (Psalm 139:7).

The Holy Spirit has a unique ministry. After Jesus died, He rose from the grave, and He remained on earth for 40 days ministering to His followers. Then Jesus physically returned to heaven. However, He did not leave His disciples and all future believers without someone to guide them. He gave them this promise: "The Advocate, the Holy Spirit, whom the Father will send in my name, will teach you all things and will remind you of everything I have said to you" (John 14:26).

Just as Jesus promised, the Holy Spirit was sent as the "Helper" (NKJV) to facilitate spiritual birth and to indwell those who experience this birth. The Holy Spirit will remain on Earth, indwelling believers and guiding them until Jesus returns.

It's interesting to note the difference the Holy Spirit can make in our lives. Before Jesus returned to heaven, He told the disciples, "You will receive power when the Holy Spirit comes on you; and you will be my witnesses" (Acts 1:8). Before the Spirit arrived, the disciples were a small group of frightened men who fled from the crucifixion and hid themselves in an upper room. But after the coming of the Spirit, their courage took a dramatic upturn. The small band of followers, empowered by the Spirit, burst into the city of Jerusalem and began to minister powerfully to the people around them.

The Holy Spirit is a helper, not a force. The Holy Spirit is the very presence of God within us. He is our helper, not an impersonal force. His personhood is evident by the fact that when sin controls us, we "grieve the Holy Spirit" (Ephesians 4:29-31). The Spirit is also quenched when we stifle the use of our spiritual gifts to Christ's body, the church (1 Thessalonians 5:19). That the Spirit grieves and can be quenched indicates He is a person.

The Holy Spirit enables us with spiritual gifts. Every believer is equipped, by the Holy Spirit, to serve others in the church. We are all gifted in various ways for the benefit of fellow believers: "There are different kinds of gifts, but the same Spirit distributes them. There are different kinds of service, but the same Lord. There are different kinds of working, but in all of them and in everyone it is the same God at work. Now to each one the manifestation of the Spirit is given for the common good" (1 Corinthians 12:4-7). Note that all the gifts are for use in the church "for the common good." Some are gifted as leaders, others as evangelists, and still others as pastors and teachers (Ephesians 4:11), while other gifts are for living in Christlike conduct, like showing mercy and helping those in need.

The Holy Spirit promotes Christlike conduct. When a person believes in Jesus Christ and comes into the family of God, he is a new person. That's why becoming a Christian is often called being "born again." This new birth is an instantaneous act in which a person receives a righteous standing before God.

As a believer, you have the Holy Spirit living in you. His ministry is to help you grow holier. Theologians refer to this growth process as "sanctification." When you allow God's Spirit to help you, the world will see the life of Jesus in your actions. How does this happen? When you "walk by the Spirit" (Galatians 5:16)—that is, when you live under the Spirit's control—you will not act in an ungodly way. Rather, you will exhibit Christlike behavior. Galatians 5:22-23 lists the character qualities that are exhibited when a person is controlled by the Spirit. These qualities are known as "the fruit of the Spirit," and they are "love, joy, peace, forbearance, kindness, goodness, faithfulness, gentleness and self-control."

The Holy Spirit is an intercessor. You may be familiar with the intercession Jesus performs for believers as He sits at the right hand of the Father (Romans 8:34). But the Holy Spirit is also an intercessor. The apostle Paul speaks of the Spirit's intercessory ministry in Romans 8:26: "In the same way, the Spirit helps us in our weakness. We do not know what we ought to pray for, but the Spirit himself intercedes for us through wordless groans."

What an amazing promise! You have the assurance that when you do not know how to pray, the Holy Spirit will pray and intercede for you so the Lord's will may be done (verse 27).

What Does This Mean for You?

An understanding of the work and ministry of the Holy Spirit is vital to your growth as a believer. It is through the Holy Spirit that God is made personal in your life. It is through the Spirit that you experience God. It is through His work that you know God's presence within you.

You also see His influence as you respond to Him in obedience. He illuminates your understanding of spiritual things when you read the Bible. He empowers your ministry through the spiritual gifts He gives you for service. And He also guarantees your future inheritance in heaven: "When you believed, you were marked in him with a seal, the promised Holy Spirit, who is a deposit guaranteeing our inheritance until the redemption of those who are God's possession—to the praise of his glory" (Ephesians 1:13-14).

8

Jesus Is Alive and Well on Planet Earth

*He who believes in Me, the works that I do, he
will do also; and greater works than these
he will do; because I go to the Father
(John 14:12 NASB).*

*Just as a body, though one, has many parts, but all its
many parts form one body, so it is with Christ. For
we were all baptized by one Spirit so as to form one
body...and we were all given the one Spirit to drink.
Even so the body is not made up of one part but of many
(1 Corinthians 12:12-14).*

*Christ is the head of the church, his
body, of which he is the Savior
(Ephesians 5:23).*

When you think of churches, what comes to mind? Many of us immediately think of beautiful old buildings with ornate trim and lots of stained glass windows. And usually one of the stained glass windows features an image of Jesus.

Unfortunately, many of the artistic images that have been created of Jesus depict Him hanging on a cross, either dead or dying.

That can cause some people to go to church with the attitude that they're going to a funeral. For them, Jesus is still hanging on a cross as a tragic historical figure. They are like the women who came to the tomb looking for the body of Jesus, which had already risen from the grave.

So how are we to view Jesus?

Jesus is not among the dead. When some of Jesus' followers came to the tomb on Sunday morning looking for His body, angels who were nearby said, "Why do you look for the living among the dead? He is not here; he has risen!" (Luke 24:5-6). Jesus is alive. He was raised from the dead and appeared to many of His followers and disciples for the next 40 days. Yes, Jesus is definitely alive! What is the proof that He is among the living? And where do you look for signs of His presence and power? Read on...

Jesus is not to be found in a building. People go to a church building thinking they will find Jesus in that place. They are like the ancient Greeks and Romans who believed their gods were found in temples built for them. The apostle Paul explained to these ancients—and to modern-day worshippers as well—that this is not true regarding Jesus. Paul said, "The God who made the world and everything in it is the Lord of heaven and earth and does not live in temples built by human hands" (Acts 17:24).

Jesus is to be found in the lives of His followers, His church. When Jesus said He would build His church (Matthew 16:18), He was not speaking of literal stones placed one upon another to form a building. He was not speaking of a physical building, but a "living organism" made up of "living stones"—of believers in Christ (1 Peter 2:5). Jesus reigns in the hearts of His followers through His church, of which He is the head. In the Bible, the church, which is made up of Christians, is described as the "body of Christ" (1 Corinthians 12:27). The church then is the living Christ in action through believers as they move throughout their communities displaying Him to a watching world.

Jesus' ministry is multiplied through His followers. When Jesus came to Earth, He took on a human body. He became a man who lived with human limitations. As a man, He could be in only one place at a time. He told His disciples that with His departure back to heaven, they would do "greater works" than He did (John 14:12 NASB). Just before Jesus returned to heaven, He explained what He meant by "greater works" when He said, "You will receive power when the Holy Spirit comes on you; and you will be my witnesses...to the ends of the earth" (Acts 1:8). Their greater works were not of the kind done by Jesus, works like miracles. Rather, the "greater works" were the greater number of disciples who took Jesus' message of salvation to the far corners of the world. As a believer today, you are a part of that great army of witnesses participating in this greater work.

Jesus' life is on display in the life of His church. Jesus, as God, lived a perfect life. His character was perfect. His actions were perfect. He was the perfect man. His followers, as members of His body, the church, are to mirror His perfect life. How does this work? When a person becomes a believer, Christ's Spirit, the Holy Spirit, comes to live in that person's heart. Then as that believer attempts to mirror Christ's character and is walking "by the Spirit," he or she will display "love, joy, peace, forbearance, kindness, goodness, faithfulness, gentleness and self-control " (Galatians 5:16,22-23). He or she will exhibit Christlikeness.

Jesus will come again. From the day Jesus returned to heaven, His followers have been living in anticipation of His return. He told His disciples He would go to heaven to prepare a place for them, then return to take them home with Him (John 14:3). After Jesus was taken up to heaven, "two men dressed in white" said, "Men of Galilee...why do you stand here looking into the sky? This same Jesus, who has been taken from you into heaven, will come back in the same way you have seen him go into heaven" (Acts 1:10-11). "In the same way" means Jesus' return will be both personal and visible (Revelation 19:11-16).

Jesus has two purposes for returning to Earth. First, as we noted in John 14:3, Jesus is returning for His people, His faithful, His church, so He can take them back home with Him. The second reason for Jesus' return is to bring judgment upon an unbelieving world (2 Thessalonians 1:6-9).

Why did Jesus, the Son of God, come to Earth? To sacrifice Himself and make payment for the sins of mankind. Only God can make this kind of offer: "I give them eternal life, and they shall never perish; no one will snatch them out of my hand" (John 10:28). To those who have accepted His offer of eternal life, Jesus sends the Spirit, who actively works in and through their lives. To be sure, Christians don't always live as their Savior did. But even with their imperfections, the changes produced in their lives serve as living proof that Jesus is alive and well on planet Earth!

Jesus' mission is not yet complete. Today God the Father is offering eternal life to all who will believe in His Son, the Lord Jesus Christ. But there is coming a day when Jesus will return to pour out judgment on all who refuse to believe.

What Does This Mean for You?

There is a day of judgment coming. Have you accepted Jesus' offer of life—life everlasting, eternal life? If so, look daily to the heavens with great anticipation. Your Savior is coming again! And as you wait, remember that Jesus is alive and well here on Earth through the lives of His followers—through people like you. So be active in your church and participate in a ministry. Give to those who are in need and to your church ministries. "Have confidence in your leaders and submit to their authority" (Hebrews 13:17). And continue to look forward with joyous anticipation to the return of Jesus, your Savior, and seeing Him face-to-face.

9

In Jesus, All Is Forgiven

*Blessed are those whose transgressions are
forgiven, whose sins are covered
(Romans 4:7).*

*In him we have redemption through his
blood, the forgiveness of sins, in accordance
with the riches of God's grace
(Ephesians 1:7).*

*I am writing to you, dear children, because your
sins have been forgiven on account of his name
(1 John 2:12).*

Christmas is a festive and joyous time of the year. And, as your bank account will testify, gift-giving is a prominent element of the holiday season!

If you are like most people, each Christmas you probably receive a few gifts with no apparent usefulness. Perhaps your Aunt Mabel gave you a sweater that doesn't fit, and it isn't even a color that looks good on you. And what about that bottle of aftershave or perfume? The odor was so strong it would make flowers wilt! Gifts like these are given by well-meaning friends and family, but hopefully you saved the original boxes so you could return them as soon as possible.

And then you also receive gifts that you love and find useful. For example, that shirt or sweater that you wore until it became a rag. And you're still using that power tool or food mixer.

But there is one Christmas gift that is of infinite worth—a gift that will never wear out. It is a most cherished and useful gift—even a life-saving one! That is the gift of God's Son, the Lord Jesus Christ. The apostle Paul called God's gift of Jesus "his indescribable gift" (2 Corinthians 9:15).

Tragically, as children of Adam and Eve, you and I and all mankind were born in rebellion against God. God is holy, and as one of the prophets in the Old Testament testified, God's "eyes are too pure to look on evil; [he] cannot tolerate wrongdoing" (Habakkuk 1:13). Therefore, for us to have a personal relationship with God, the event of the cross had to take place (2 Corinthians 5:21).

When people receive God's gift of Jesus, they receive a key benefit—God's forgiveness: "In him we have redemption through his blood, the forgiveness of sins, in accordance with the riches of God's grace" (Ephesians 1:7). What is involved in God's forgiveness?

God's forgiveness is complete. It's important to note that when a person receives Jesus Christ and is born into the family of God, their sins are forgiven once and for all. When Jesus declared "It is finished" on the cross, He was speaking of His work of redemption (John 19:30). Jesus died for your sins and mine. Every sin that you and I will ever commit is covered by Jesus' death.

Christian, as God's child, His forgiveness of you is complete because Jesus' work is completed. God's justice was satisfied, and complete forgiveness is yours.

God's forgiveness is permanent. You can probably still remember a particularly painful thing that someone did to you in the past. Maybe you have forgiven that person of that wrong, and you are trying to forget about what happened. But the pain is still there, and you still remember what took place.

When it comes to forgiveness, God is not like us. When He forgives, He also forgets. Psalm 103:12 says, "As far as the east is from the west, so far has he removed our transgressions from us." When a person thoroughly forsakes their sins, God thoroughly forgives him and remembers his sins no more.

God's forgiveness is unending. You've likely heard the expression "a gift that keeps on giving." That perfectly describes God's forgiveness through His Son. Whether our sins are few or many, or whether they are big or small, God has forgiven them. God's ability to forgive all our sins does not give us license to deliberately mess up, but it does encourage us to know that when we do fail, we don't need to fear that God's grace will cease. God is not a policeman, but our Father. In Jesus, you and I are adopted sons and daughters, and because His forgiveness is eternal, our status as His children is eternal as well.

God's forgiveness is to be shared. One of the greatest blessings of God's forgiveness is the opportunity we have to pass that same mercy on to others (Matthew 5:7). God has forgiven us of so much—shouldn't we do the same for others?

At this point you may be thinking as Peter did when he asked Jesus, "Lord, how many times shall I forgive my brother or sister who sins against me? Up to seven times?" Jesus responded, "I tell you, not seven times, but seventy-seven times" (Matthew 18:21-22). In other words, Jesus is saying that our forgiveness should be limitless.

A willingness to forgive others is a key identifying mark of a true believer. Forgiveness from God is man's deepest need, and forgiveness of others is man's highest achievement. And such forgiveness should begin in our own home, toward those who are closest to us.

God's forgiveness is consistent. God never changes. He has promised forgiveness and supplies it the moment a person receives Christ as Savior. And with that forgiveness will come the desire to avoid sin and stay pure for the Lord.

While it's true that God forgives sin, it's also true that He overlooks none. So when you do sin, you should immediately confess that sin, knowing that God is faithful to extend His forgiveness to us. That's what 1 John 1:9 talks about: "If we confess our sins, he is faithful and just and will forgive us our sins and purify us from all unrighteousness." Ours is a dynamic relationship with God. As we continue to confess, He continues to forgive. Confession is not a condition for God's forgiveness, but a result of it.

God's forgiveness should change you. It's wonderful that God's forgiveness is complete, permanent, and limitless. But we need to be careful we don't take advantage of His forgiveness and assume He will overlook sin in our lives. Each act of forgiveness is an opportunity to learn a lesson, and learn how to avoid the same sin in the future. Not only should we confess every sin as quickly as possible, but we should ask God for His wisdom and strength in resisting sin. The fact He is faithful to forgive should motivate us toward holy living.

What Does This Mean for You?

Many believers struggle with some sin they think is too big for God to forgive. If this describes you, remember that God's grace is bigger than all your sin. Sure, there may be some fallout you will have to deal with in the aftermath. Broken relationships are hard to mend. Broken laws have their just penalties. Borrowed and mismanaged money must be repaid. However, God's cleansing love and forgiveness can see you through any and all consequences.

If you haven't experienced God's forgiveness, it all starts with receiving God's gift—Jesus Christ. Accept His forgiveness, embrace His mercy, and trust in His powerful promise that His forgiveness is forever. What a Savior!

10

You Are Worth More Than You Think

When I consider your heavens, the work of your fingers,
the moon and the stars, which you have set in place,
what is mankind that you are mindful of them, human
beings that you care for them? You have made them a
little lower than the angels and crowned them with
glory and honor. You made them rulers over the works
of your hands; you put everything under their feet
(Psalm 8:3–6).

I praise you because I am fearfully and wonderfully made;
your works are wonderful, I know that full well. My frame
was not hidden from you when I was made in the secret
place, when I was woven together in the depths of the earth.
Your eyes saw my unformed body; all the days ordained for
me were written in your book before one of them came to be
(Psalm 139:14–16).

Many people suffer from what has been labeled by some as low self-esteem or low self-image. For whatever reason, they don't think very highly of themselves. They don't like how they look, or they feel inadequate in one way or another. Many of them let their perceptions of themselves affect them to the point they withdraw into a shell of sadness and loneliness. Others try to compensate for their perceived shortcomings by putting on a mask of self-assurance or making themselves into someone they are not.

But God's desire is for us to view ourselves through His eyes. To Him, we have great worth. This is the answer to any self-esteem problems we might have. After you finish this chapter, you just might come to realize that *you are worth more than you think!*

Your worth is grounded in creation. Early in our marriage, my wife and I designed and built a pine bookcase. She designed it and I built it. Then we stained our "creation." For the next 30 years, that bookcase was the focal point in our family room everywhere we lived. From a monetary standpoint it was practically worthless, costing us only about $30 in materials. But because we had made it, the bookcase was priceless to us.

From a purely physical standpoint, the human body is made up of materials worth very little. But to God, you are priceless. Why? Because He created you. "God created mankind in his own image, in the image of God he created them; male and female he created them" (Genesis 1:27). Just as our pine bookcase was special to us, so God has declared that you are special to Him, even before you were born: "Your eyes saw my unformed body; all the days ordained for me were written in your book before one of them came to be" (Psalm 139:16).

Doesn't it follow that if you are priceless to the Creator of the universe, you should not think poorly of yourself? You should never think of yourself as worthless or useless if you claim a relationship to the great God who made you.

Your worth is measured by God's sovereign care. Jesus masterfully drove this point home in one of His teachings. Even when a single seemingly insignificant sparrow falls to the ground, it does not happen "outside your Father's care," or apart from the Father's knowledge (Matthew 10:29). Jesus then pointed out that if God is so concerned about one little sparrow, how much more do you think He is concerned about you? The answer? More—much more! Jesus said, "You are worth more than many sparrows" (verse 31).

And Jesus didn't stop there. You and all believers are so

important to your Father that He has numbered "even the very hairs of your head" (verse 30). What's your worth to God? Medical experts estimate there are more than 100,000 hair follicles on the human scalp, and that the average man loses—and sprouts— about 100 hairs a day. This probably also applies to women. It's truly amazing that God has your every hair numbered. That's how important you are to Him.

Your worth is determined by your closeness to Jesus. Some people suffer from a low self-image because they erroneously think they aren't worth anything to anybody. Others have just the opposite problem—they have a huge ego and think there is nothing they can't do. They think they are worth everything! Notice that both types of people have their focus on *themselves* and their own abilities or lack of them.

As a Christian, you must realize that your worth comes from Jesus Christ alone. He said, "I am the vine; you are the branches. If you remain in me and I in you, you will bear much fruit; apart from me you can do nothing" (John 15:5). The basis of your worth is your identity in and with Christ. It's that simple and that fantastic. Apart from Him, by eternal standards, you are incapable of accomplishing anything.

From a human standpoint, there are many men and women who are successful. That's because we measure success in terms of annual salary, square footage of a home, level of education, job stature, talent, physical beauty, professional standing. But true worth comes only when you abide in Christ and stay closely connected with Him. Jesus alone is truly worthy, and it is in Him, in Christ, that you possess your worth. There is no greater worth than to have Christ living and working through you! "I have been crucified with Christ and I no longer live, but Christ lives in me" (Galatians 2:20).

Your worth has a purpose. You are special to God because you are His creation. That you are special to Him is proven by the fact that God, in His grace, reached out and saved you (Ephesians 2:8-9). For what purpose? "[You] are God's handiwork, created in Christ Jesus to do good works, which God prepared in advance for [you] to do" (verse 10). He also put His Spirit in you and gave you unique spiritual gifts so you could serve Him and His people: "Now to each one the manifestation of the Spirit is given for the common good" (1 Corinthians 12:7).

These spiritual gifts are special abilities you possess so you can minister to the needs of fellow believers. Other believers are depending on you to use your gifts to strengthen and encourage them. You are worth something to all believers!

What Does This Mean for You?

God's Word repeatedly assures you of your worth to God. He created you. He gave His Son to die for your sins. He placed His Holy Spirit in you to guide and instruct you. And He has promised that someday you will live forever with Him in heaven. God has definitely done His part to prove you are valuable to Him. Now, it's your turn:

—Be thankful to God for choosing you as one of His special people.

—View any limitations you think you have as opportunities to trust God. Depend on Him and His strength in the midst of your weaknesses.

—Remember that your worth is not based on *you* and what *you* can do, but on *God* and what *He* has done—and will do.

11

Caring for Those in Need Is One of God's Top Priorities

Whoever oppresses the poor shows contempt for their Maker, but whoever is kind to the needy honors God (Proverbs 14:31).

Whoever is kind to the poor lends to the LORD, and he will reward them for what they have done (Proverbs 19:17).

The generous will themselves be blessed, for they share their food with the poor (Proverbs 22:9).

Compassion and mercy are fundamental pillars of the Christian faith. Repeatedly throughout the Old Testament we see God demonstrate His concern for those in need, whether it was through Jewish laws that allowed the poor to glean the grain left behind during harvest (Ruth 2), or through special means, such as when the prophet Elisha took care of a starving widow (1 Kings 17:9).

God, in His mercy, is concerned for those who are poor and suffering. In James 1:27, God identifies true religion by its concern for the less fortunate: "Religion that God our Father accepts as pure and faultless is this: to look after orphans and widows in their distress." If we are to identify with our heavenly Father, we too must express genuine concern for others.

Caring is a Godlike quality. According to Genesis 1:26, we read that God created man "in His own image." Obviously man is not a god, but being made in the image of God gives man some of God's attributes. We have the opportunity to exhibit certain Godlike characteristics, like compassion: "Because of the LORD's great love we are not consumed, for his compassions never fail" (Lamentations 3:22). The unfailing love of God never ends. This same compassion that has been offered to us as image-bearers of God should, in turn, be offered to others.

Jesus demonstrated God's concern for others. During His three years of ministry, Jesus spent much of His time helping the sick, the dying, and the destitute. For example, in one instance, we read that "the people brought to Jesus all the sick and demon-possessed. The whole town gathered at the door" (Mark 1:32-33).

God expects us to care for those in need. Jesus was known for telling parables that communicated important truths. On one occasion He told a story about a king (depicting Himself) who returned to reclaim His throne. To one group of His subjects He said, "Come, you who are blessed by my Father; take your inheritance, the kingdom prepared for you since the creation of the world. For I was hungry and you gave me something to eat, I was thirsty and you gave me something to drink, I was a stranger and you invited me in, I needed clothes and you clothed me, I was sick and you looked after me, I was in prison and you came to visit me" (Matthew 25:34-36).

The king's loyal subjects were mystified. The king had been away in a far country and they couldn't remember offering him this kind of care. The king then said, "Truly I tell you, whatever you did for one of the least of these brothers and sisters of mine, you did for me" (verse 40). The message is clear: When we care for the needy, we are doing it in Jesus' place.

Compassion is unnatural. You are probably familiar with the story of the Good Samaritan in Luke 10:25-37. Jesus tells of a man who was beaten, robbed, and left for dead. Three different travelers passed by the poor man as he lay on the road. Two of them ignored the man, but the third one—a Samaritan—stopped, cared for the man, took him to an inn, and paid for him to stay there until he was well enough to travel again.

Unfortunately the response of the first two travelers is seen in many today when they cross paths with people in need. Even Christians who have been shown mercy and compassion from God will sometimes withhold their compassion. That's because compassion doesn't come naturally for us. Rather, it requires a deliberate act of the will—that's why we are commanded, "Clothe yourselves with compassion, kindness, humility, gentleness and patience" (Colossians 3:12). If the apostle Paul found it necessary to make this a command, that means compassion is not an automatic response! We must work at this Godlike quality and care for those in need.

Caring should produce kindness. It is assumed that if you care about a person's need, you will do something about it. A person could say, "I care about those who are suffering" yet do nothing. God always follows through on His care and concern, and He expects us to do the same. Besides compassion, Christians are to also clothe themselves with kindness (Colossians 3:12). A heart that genuinely cares should respond with kindness.

Caring is contagious. As a Christian, your sense of caring should not be based on guilt, or even pity. It should be based on love, and more specifically, Christ's love flowing through you into the lives of those in need. The apostle Paul was a strongly driven, highly focused man with a singular mission—the preaching of the gospel. He had a Type A personality. But he was also a loving and caring shepherd of the people around him. For example, hear his concern as he pours out his heart to the elders of the church at Ephesus: "I served the Lord with great humility and with tears and in the midst of severe testing by the plots of my Jewish opponents. You know that I have not hesitated to preach anything that would be helpful to you but have taught you publicly and from house to house" (Acts 20:19-20).

What was the result of Paul's love and care for the people? They returned his love. First, the church leaders walked 30-plus miles to say good-bye as Paul was on his way to Jerusalem. Second, "when Paul had finished his speech," they all wept and embraced him and kissed him. What grieved them most was his statement that they would never see his face again. Then they accompanied him to the ship (verses 37-38).

What Does This Mean for You?

When it comes to compassion and caring, it always helps to think of Jesus. Use these scriptures and incidents from Jesus' ministry as a checklist for your compassion and care for others. As a child of God with a relationship with His Son, Jesus, and the Holy Spirit living in you, you can produce the fruit of love, kindness, and goodness that was on display in Jesus' life.

— Jesus went about doing good (Acts 10:38).

— Jesus was moved with compassion when the people had no food and arranged to feed them (Matthew 14:14).

— Jesus stopped to help the helpless, like the blind man, the lame man, the woman with the bent back, and the widow who had lost her son.

Who needs your help today? Your prayers? Your provision? You will have the greatest impact on others when you give yourself away to others.

12

We Should Forgive Just as We Are Forgiven

Peter came to Jesus and asked, "Lord, how many times shall I forgive my brother or sister who sins against me? Up to seven times?" Jesus answered, "I tell you, not seven times, but seventy-seven times" (Matthew 18:21-22).

In him we have redemption through his blood, the forgiveness of sins, in accordance with the riches of God's grace (Ephesians 1:7).

Bear with each other and forgive one another if any of you has a grievance against someone. Forgive as the Lord forgave you (Colossians 3:13).

The Hatfields and McCoys. The mere mention of these names stirs up visions of violence and an unwillingness to forgive. This famous feud was between two families who lived in the area between Kentucky and West Virginia. The feud began in 1865 with the murder of one of the McCoys. Over the next 35 years, the two families traded murders and violence. The feud eventually faded into history with the death of both family leaders in the early years

of the twentieth century. Although the conflict subsided genera-
tions ago, the names Hatfield and McCoy still conjure in people's
mind an attitude of vengeance and an unwillingness to forgive.

The Hatfields and McCoys are not the only families who have
exhibited ongoing hostility. There are many people—even Christians—who view themselves as victims who are justified in carry-
ing out vengeance. And unfortunately, one act of retaliation can
end up fueling the fires of retaliation from the other side. And thus
a cycle is set into motion that can last for weeks, months, or even
years. What is the solution? One word: forgiveness!

Forgiveness is not the natural response. What is the typical
response when someone—including you!—is wronged? Usually
our first thought is for vengeance. Think back to when you were a
child. When someone hit you, your first instinct was to hit them
back—or at least, you wanted to! And if you were caught in the act,
you'd holler, "He hit me first!"

How do you refrain from retaliating when you are wronged?
First, realize that vengeance, or any kind of payback, is sin. When
people hurt you, instead of giving them what you think they deserve,
follow the apostle Paul's advice: "Do not repay anyone evil for evil.
Be careful to do what is right in the eyes of everyone. If it is possible, as far as it depends on you, live at peace with everyone. Do
not take revenge, my dear friends, but leave room for God's wrath,
for it is written: 'It is mine to avenge; I will repay,' says the Lord"
(Romans 12:16-19).

Forgiveness follows God's pattern. In spite of what people may
think or believe, God is a forgiving God. Throughout the Old Testament, God repeatedly forgave the transgressions of His people.
In the New Testament, we see this forgiveness spelled out very
clearly in passages like Ephesians 1:7: "In him we have redemption through his blood, the forgiveness of sins, in accordance with
the riches of God's grace." This forgiveness is called "God's grace."
Grace is defined as receiving something that is undeserved. We
don't deserve God's forgiveness, yet His grace gives it anyway.

The Bible tells us that because God has forgiven us, we should be willing to forgive others. Colossians 3:13 says we are to "bear with each other and forgive one another if any of you has a grievance against someone. Forgive as the Lord forgave you."

Forgiveness is an act of the will. As with other heart attitudes like love, joy, and peace, forgiveness is a deliberate choice. When it comes to being hurt by others, you have a decision to make: Will I love this person or not? Will I choose to have joy even in the midst of this joyless situation or not? And, will I choose to forgive this person or not?

In every conflict, the people involved have a choice. Will they forgive the other party? If you have been wronged by another person, choose to take the godly path. Look to God for His grace and, by an act of your will, choose to show forgiveness.

Forgiveness does not have a memory. Sinful vengeance keeps records. It waits for the right time to retaliate. But sometimes people who forgive also want to keep records. Jesus faced this problem with His disciples. The Jewish teachers of that day taught that people should forgive others who offended them—but only three times.

Peter, one of the disciples, wanted to make himself look good by being even more generous about forgiveness. So he asked Jesus: "'Lord, how many times shall I forgive my brother or sister who sins against me? Up to seven times?' Jesus answered, 'I tell you, not seven times, but seventy-seven times'" (Matthew 18:21-22). Jesus' answer is surprising. Christians should be willing to forgive other people an unlimited number of times! In other words, we should not keep track of how many times someone hurts us or how many times we forgive that person.

Forgiveness inspires forgiveness. A forgiven person is a forgiving person. If you have experienced God's forgiving grace for all your wrongs, you should pass that grace on to others. When you realize who you were before Christ came into your life and extended His forgiveness to you, and where you were headed without God's forgiveness, you should find it easier to forgive a wrong inflicted on you by another person.

Unfortunately, we often forget what it means to be forgiven, and refuse to forgive others. An unforgiving attitude is a sinful attitude. Such an attitude affects your fellowship with others and especially with God. Jesus made it clear that our willingness to forgive others is interrelated with receiving forgiveness from God: "If you forgive other people when they sin against you, your heavenly Father will also forgive you. But if you do not forgive others their sins, your Father will not forgive your sins" (Matthew 6:14-15).

What Does This Mean for You?

As a believer in Christ, you have been forgiven. When you refuse to forgive others, you don't lose your salvation, but you do lose your fellowship with God. Your fellowship with God is too high a price to pay for not forgiving others.

The Bible says, "As far as the east is from the west, so far has he removed our transgressions from us" (Psalm 103:12). By saying "east is from the west," the psalmist was saying, "God completely removed your sins. They are gone and can never be found!" And because God has forgiven all your sins, you should not withhold forgiveness from others.

13

Prayer Is a Way You Can Connect with God

*Do not be anxious about anything, but in
every situation, by prayer and petition, with
thanksgiving, present your requests to God
(Philippians 4:6).*

*Pray continually, give thanks in all circumstances;
for this is God's will for you in Christ Jesus
(1 Thessalonians 5:17–18).*

*Devote yourselves to prayer, being watchful and thankful
(Colossians 4:2).*

My wife Elizabeth and I happen to live in a house that sits on a hill. That means our home was built with several split levels. Each day one of us writes on one level in the house and the other writes on another. To communicate with each other from office to office while we're working on our manuscripts, we use walkie-talkies.

One day when our grandchildren were with us, they spotted the walkie-talkies and, of course, they wanted to talk on them. After explaining how they worked, we gave one to Jacob and the other to Katie, ages five and four years old respectively. Well, it wasn't long before both children came back, walkie-talkies in hand, crying and complaining that they were broken—they didn't work! Because they were too young to understand how to send and receive messages, Jacob and Katie were sure the problem was with the walkie-talkies.

Surprisingly, when it comes to communicating with God, many Christians are like our grandchildren. They don't understand how to communicate with their heavenly Father. As a result, when their prayers seemingly aren't being answered, they tend to get discouraged and blame God. They think He is the problem. They ask, "Why isn't God answering my prayers?" In many cases, they give up and quit trying to pray.

It's when we have a right understanding of what prayer is that we are not so quick to blame God for what we think is unanswered prayer or assume that God doesn't hear us. The key is knowing how to pray and the purpose of prayer.

Prayer is worship—In the Old Testament, much of the worship carried out by God's people was related to the sacrificial system set down by God's law. These sacrificial acts of the worshippers were associated with and accompanied by prayer—by making an entreaty to God. As the aroma of the sacrifices went up from the altar, prayers also ascended to God.

As New Testament worshippers, you and I don't kill and burn animals or offer incense as a sacrifice to the Lord. God calls us to offer up a different kind of sacrifice—that of personal prayer. We are to lift our prayers to Him. We are to offer the "incense" of our prayers. And unlike the Old Testament worshippers, who had prescribed places and times for offering sacrifices, we can offer up our sacrifice of prayer anywhere and at any time! In prayer, we are offering the sacrifice of...

> our will for God's will,
>
> our neglect for God's attention,
>
> our sin for God's forgiveness;
>
> our callous heart for God's loving heart.

Prayer is talking to God—What is the best way to communicate with others? While the various types of social media or texting are popular today, the best way to communicate is by talking, either by phone or face-to-face. This is exactly how God wants you to communicate with Him. He wants you to "ask and it will be given to you; seek and you will find; knock and the door will be opened to you" (Matthew 7:7). And the nice thing about talking to God is there are no dead zones and no roaming charges—and no voice mail! Best of all, God is always there to receive your call 24/7.

Prayer acknowledges your trust in God—When we don't pray, we are basically saying we doubt that prayer makes a difference. We are showing that we don't trust in God's promise that "you may ask me anything in My name, and I will do it" (John 14:14). If you are having difficulty with trusting God and His promises about prayer, then start with simple prayer requests. Be faithful. Pray every day. Keep it up, and watch your faith grow as you see God working in your life. Then when the big issues come along, your faith in prayer and God's wisdom and guidance will be mature enough to handle the answers God gives you.

Prayer is an opportunity to bring your will into line with God's plans—Communicating with God through prayer doesn't mean you demand what you want. Rather, it is your opportunity to talk things over with God, always keeping in mind that ultimately, you are trying to better understand the mind of God. God has His reasons for how He is working in your life. You cannot nor should you try to change God's perfect plan for you. Your job in prayer is to discuss with Him what He wants for you. And what happens when you align your prayers to His will? "This is the confidence we have in approaching God: that if we ask anything according to his will, he hears us" (1 John 5:14).

Prayer restores relationships—Sin in your life affects your relationships—with your spouse, your children, your family, your friends, and especially God. Your sin puts a wall of separation between you and God. Whatever the situation, it can be salvaged if you are willing to turn to God. No matter how long or far you have drifted away from God, He is ready to hear from you and restore you to a right relationship with Him. Then, with His help and grace, you can restore your relationships with others.

Prayer needs to be a constant in your life—The popular saying, "Absence makes the heart grow fonder" is not true. Instead, absence strains a relationship. Absence can easily diminish or even extinguish a relationship. It is only as you and the other person get close and stay close that your love and appreciation for each other has the opportunity to blossom and grow.

It's the same way with your relationship with God. The more time you spend with God in prayer, the closer your relationship becomes. That's why Christians are admonished to "devote yourselves to prayer," and "pray continually, give thanks in all circumstances" (Colossians 4:2; 1 Thessalonians 5:17-18). Close the gap—take a simple step and talk to God, not as an afterthought, but as your first thought. The more you talk to God, the closer you'll get to the heart and mind of God.

Prayer is being offered for you even when you don't know how to pray—God does answer your prayers! In fact, He promises to answer you even when you don't know how to pray about a certain issue. As Romans 8:26 says, "The Spirit helps us in our weakness. We do not know what we ought to pray for, but the Spirit himself intercedes for us." Just as a close friend is always there to hear your heartfelt concerns, God is more so.

What Does This Mean for You?

It really is true that prayer changes things. While you won't necessarily understand how prayer works in connection with God's sovereign will, somehow your prayers really do have a part in God working out His will in your life. As I mentioned earlier in this book, you don't need to know how a computer works to take advantage of its usefulness. Neither are you required to know how prayer works! All you need to know is that your Savior wants you to play a part in His grand plan by praying. He wants you to pray daily, often, and with passion. "Ask and it will be given to you; seek and you will find; knock and the door will be opened to you. For everyone who asks receives; the one who seeks finds; and to the one who knocks, the door will be opened" (Matthew 7:7-9).

14

You Are Made to Live Forever

*God so loved the world that he gave his one
and only Son, that whoever believes in him
shall not perish but have eternal life
(John 3:16).*

*Now this is eternal life: that they know you, the only
true God, and Jesus Christ, whom you have sent
(John 17:3).*

*The world and its desires pass away, but
whoever does the will of God lives forever
(1 John 2:17).*

Ponce de León, a sixteenth-century Spanish explorer, spent his life searching for the Fountain of Youth. Obviously he did not succeed. But he did discover the state of Florida. Tales of a Fountain of Youth had been circulating for a long time. This fountain was supposedly able to restore the youth of anyone who drank or bathed in its waters. That enticed Ponce de León—after all, who wouldn't want to remain eternally young?

The prospect of living forever is a concept that is at the heart of many religions. Even people who say they are not religious would dearly love to possess eternal life because they are afraid of death. But for Christians, eternal life is a sure thing, and a fundamental element of our beliefs. Here's how eternal life is described in the Bible:

Eternal life was forfeited at the Fall. Man was created in God's image. God breathed life into man, and man became a living being. This didn't make man a god. It simply meant that man possessed some of the attributes of God, like emotion, intellect, and the ability to reason. After man was created, he was placed in the Garden of Eden in a state of untested holiness. Theoretically, if the man Adam had not sinned, he would have lived forever in that condition.

God gave Adam one prohibition: "You must not eat from the tree of the knowledge of good and evil." What would happen if man disobeyed? God said, "You will certainly die" (Genesis 2:17). Death would come to man, beginning with spiritual death. Yet Adam did what God said he was not to do: He ate from the tree of the knowledge of good and evil. By sinning against God, Adam forfeited eternal life. Through Adam's sin, death was brought into the world. Does this mean eternal life was lost? No—God's grace would restore the possibility of eternal life to fallen mankind.

Eternal life cannot be earned. A rich young ruler asked Jesus, "Good teacher, what must I do to inherit eternal life?" (Luke 18:18). This young man wanted Jesus to give him a set of rules to keep and tasks to perform in order to ensure his own immortality. He wanted to know how he could earn eternal life. No formula was offered by Jesus because salvation and eternal life cannot be earned. Eternal life is God's gift: "It is by grace you have been saved, through faith— and this is not from yourselves, it is the gift of God—not by works, so that no one can boast" (Ephesians 2:8-9).

Eternal life begins in this life. Because of our sin problem, we are separated from God. Jesus said that to enter God's kingdom, "You must be born again" (John 3:7). It is at the moment of salvation, when God's Spirit enters into a person, that eternal life begins. That person will eventually go on to die physically, but their soul will live on for all eternity in the presence of Christ.

Eternal life is yours through Jesus Christ. There are many religions and philosophies that speak of eternal life. People like Ponce de León search everywhere in the hopes of finding eternal life, and miss the one true source. The answer is simple: "Whoever has the Son has life; whoever does not have his Son does not have life" (1 John 5:12).

Jesus is all you need. Eternal life is yours the moment you believe in Jesus Christ as Savior. You don't need to work for it because it is a gift. You don't need to worry about losing it because you have been sealed with the Holy Spirit (Ephesians 4:30)—He is your guarantee of eternal life.

Eternal life can be a certainty. There is much uncertainty in this world. Maybe you're experiencing uncertainty right now—about your health, your job, your family, your finances, your future, and especially your eternal future. Only Christians can say with certainty they have eternal life. The apostle John wrote, "I write these things to you who believe in the name of the Son of God so that you may know that you have eternal life" (1 John 5:13).

How can you know you have eternal life? John says you need to believe in the Son of God—Jesus Christ. The first Adam plunged mankind into spiritual death. But when you enter into a personal relationship with the second Adam—with Jesus—you can know for certain that you are a partaker of His eternal life. "God has given us eternal life, and this life is in his Son" (1 John 5:11).

Eternal life cannot be lost. Adam lost everlasting life when he sinned. As a result, all of Adam's posterity, including you, are spiritually dead (Romans 5:12). But with the death and resurrection of Jesus Christ as the second Adam, we can regain that life, "for as in Adam all die, so in Christ all will be made alive... The first man Adam became a living being; the last Adam, a life-giving spirit" (1 Corinthians 15:22,45).

When you receive Jesus as your Savior, He ensures your eternal position with Him by giving you His Spirit. The Bible explains, "When you believed, you were marked in him with a seal, the promised Holy Spirit, who is a deposit guaranteeing our inheritance until the redemption of those who are God's possession—to the praise of his glory" (Ephesians 1:13-14). The Spirit's presence in you is your guarantee of the security of your salvation!

Eternal life is a curse for some. Up to now, we have talked about eternal life as a desirable concept. Who wouldn't want to live forever? Many people spend their whole life searching for the possibility of some kind of eternal existence. If you are a believer in Jesus Christ, you possess this glorious prospect!

For others, however, the concept of eternal life is a curse. They will not look forward to it. Why? Because without Jesus, their lives are contaminated with the curse of Adam's sin. For these people, eternity will be a place where they will pay for the sins they have committed in this life—forever.

But eternity doesn't have to be this way—anyone who is not yet a believer can receive God's offer of a fresh, new existence with hope. This new start comes when a person repents of his sin and asks Christ to take control of his life. Here's how it works: "If anyone is in Christ, he is a new creation; old things have passed away; behold, all things have become new" (2 Corinthians 5:17 NKJV). Eternal life begins the moment Christ comes into your life—God's eternity becomes embedded into your heart.

What Does This Mean for You?

Thousands of years ago, Moses challenged the people of Israel to "choose life" (Deuteronomy 30:19). God is offering this life to everyone who seeks Him: "You will seek Me and find me, when you search for me with all your heart" (Jeremiah 29:13 NKJV). This life—eternal life—comes when you accept Jesus. If you have already received Jesus as your Savior, you can rest in the promise that you will live forever. Knowing that your soul will never die should give you great courage and patience as you endure whatever life sends your way.

15

Satan Is Not as Powerful as You Think He Is

The God of peace will soon crush Satan under your feet. The grace of our Lord Jesus be with you (Romans 16:20).

The reason the Son of God appeared was to destroy the devil's work (1 John 3:8).

He seized the dragon, that ancient serpent, who is the devil, or Satan, and bound him for a thousand years (Revelation 20:2).

The term *prelude* is commonly used to refer to a piece of music that precedes a more important or the major part of a movement in a musical composition. In terms of history, a prelude is an action or event that precedes something else, usually something bigger, larger, or grander.

Well, did you know that there was a prelude to Genesis 1:1? Before time and "the beginning" of Genesis 1:1, a prelude took place. During the period of the time that made up the prelude, God created the angelic realm (Colossians 1:16). The beings that populated this realm were spirit beings who could not die, were in a state of holiness, and possessed great power.

However, during this prelude, something tragic happened. One of the angelic beings God created—who was described as "the seal of perfection, full of wisdom and perfect in beauty" (Ezekiel 28:12), became proud and was expelled from heaven by God (verses 15-17).

When God created the material universe in Genesis chapter 1, this fallen spirit, Satan, was already in existence. This diabolical spirit took control of the body of a serpent and led mankind into sin (Genesis 3:1-7). While it's true that Satan is extremely powerful and utterly evil and commands an army of fallen angels or demons, he was and still is just one of God's many created beings. Therefore, he was and is ultimately answerable to God. In fact, because God is still sovereign over all things, Satan is not as powerful as he thinks he is. Let's look now at what the Bible says about Satan and his ultimate demise.

Satan must answer to God. There is a very informative prologue in the book of Job, in chapters 1 and 2. There, Satan challenged the character of a man named Job by attributing Job's righteous behavior to God's blessings on his life. Satan said that if God's blessings were to cease, Job would curse God. God accepted Satan's challenge and allowed Satan to test Job—with certain restrictions, of course. He said to Satan, "'Very well, then, everything he [Job] has is in your power, but on the man himself do not lay a finger.'Then Satan went out from the presence of the Lord" (Job 1:12).

As you can see, Satan had no authority over Job. He had to receive permission from God to test Job, and the test had to stay within God's set limits. Later, in the New Testament, Jesus affirmed Satan's lack of authority when He told Peter that Satan had to ask for permission to test any of God's children: "Simon, Simon, Satan has asked to sift all of you as wheat" (Luke 22:31).

All of this information is good news for you. It means that Satan has no power over you except what God permits in order to test your righteousness just as he tested Job and Peter.

Jesus came to defeat the power of Satan. When Adam and Eve sinned, they in essence switched their obedience from God to Satan. As a result, the whole world now lies in the power of the devil (1 John 5:19). As Hebrews 2:14 says, Jesus came to break that power: "Since the children have flesh and blood, he too shared in their humanity so that by his death he might break the power of him who holds the power of death—that is, the devil." The first Adam came under bondage to the power of Satan, but the last Adam—Jesus Christ—broke that power with His death as payment for mankind's sin.

Jesus set the pattern for defeating Satan. Immediately after Jesus was affirmed by the Father at His baptism, He was led into the wilderness to be tempted by the devil (Matthew 4:1). Jesus' time of testing proved He was indeed the Son of God and well able to overcome the devil and his temptations. Jesus' responses to temptation also give us an example to follow when we are tempted. Even though we are not God, we, like Jesus, can face temptation, resist it, and have victory over it. Jesus shows us the way: Each time He was tempted, He quoted from the written Word of God. So arm yourself with God's Word—hide it in your heart that you might not sin against God (Psalm 119:11).

Satan is waging war against believers. Satan's fight is not against an unbelieving world. The world is already his prisoner. Satan's focus is to sideline or derail believers. If he can get Christ's followers to disobey God and live in unrepentant sin, he has effectively defeated their witness and spiritual empowerment and usefulness to the cause of Christ. To withstand Satan's attacks, you must depend on God's strength and use every piece of the armor He has provided. "Put on the full armor of God, so that you can take your stand against the devil's schemes" (Ephesians 6:11). (For a full list of the pieces of your armor, see Ephesians 6:14-17.)

Satan is a defeated enemy. Satan's first defeat came when he was cast out of heaven by God. The war between God and evil rages on. Satan is continuing to fight a losing battle, and we don't have to wait to know who will win. Satan will lose in the end. We have it in writing: "The devil, who deceived them, was thrown into the lake of burning sulfur, where the beast and the false prophet had been thrown. They will be tormented day and night for ever and ever" (Revelation 20:10).

Unfortunately, for now, Satan is still active, and he continues to tempt us to doubt God. Satan is relentless in trying to persuade us to live our lives without God's help.

What Does This Mean for You?

Satan is a fallen angel who is real, and his temptations are real. He tempted Eve in the Garden of Eden, he tempted Jesus in the wilderness, and he still tempts all believers today.

When you become discouraged because it looks like evil is winning over righteousness, remember these powerful truths: Jesus defeated Satan on the cross. The penalty for sin has been paid in full. With thanks to Jesus, ultimate victory is ours. But for the time being, Satan does everything he can to get us to live his way rather than God's way. Therefore, we will face temptation frequently.

When you think you cannot resist temptation, or you find yourself rationalizing why it's okay to give in to temptation, remember: "You, dear children, are from God...the one who is in you is greater than the one who is in the world" (1 John 4:4).

16

Ignore Satan at Your Own Risk

*Be alert and of sober mind. Your enemy the devil prowls
around like a roaring lion looking for someone to devour
(1 Peter 5:8).*

*Submit yourselves, then, to God. Resist the
devil, and he will flee from you
(James 4:7).*

*The one who does what is sinful is of the devil, because
the devil has been sinning from the beginning
(1 John 3:8).*

"To be forewarned is to be forearmed" is a good motto for Christians to remember when it comes to Satan. He is to be considered Public Enemy Number One by all Christians. You might be thinking, *Wait a minute. Didn't Jesus defeat him at the cross? So why should I be so fearful? He has no power over me. I'm a Christian!*

You're right. This is absolutely true. However, Satan is still "the god of this age" (2 Corinthians 4:4), and he has the power to tempt believers. The Bible has many names for this "god of this age"—names that define Satan's activities:

Satan—to be or act as an adversary. He is the opponent, the one who opposes the cause of God and the people of God.

Devil—adversary or accuser. We get the word *diabolical* from the Greek New Testament word translated "devil."

Accuser, tempter, adversary, deceiver, father of lies, murderer, and sinner—here are a few additional names, and there are more.

All these names convey something of the character and practices of the devil. A brief study of them can give you insight into some of his tactics. In your responses to him, you need to be on guard against two extremes. First, do not take him too lightly, lest you disregard the biblical warnings. Second, do not fault him for all your misdeeds. To do that is to have a "the devil made me do it" mentality. With these cautions in mind, here are some of the devil's tactics to be aware of:

Satan's primary weapon is deception. The apostle Paul tells us that Satan disguises himself as an angel of light, and his demons also disguise themselves as servants of righteousness (2 Corinthians 11:14-15). This deception primarily involves religion. Satan has blinded the minds of unbelievers to worship false gods. He also causes unbelievers to worship the true God, but in the wrong way—through a system that centers on doing good works to obtain salvation and forgiveness.

Satan deceives Christians through false teachers, including those who use the Bible to "prove" their teachings. That's why Paul warns believers that "savage wolves will come in among you and will not spare the flock. Even from your own number men will arise and distort the truth in order to draw away disciples after them. So be on your guard!" (Acts 20:29-31).

Satan's goal is to keep Christians from knowing God. From the beginning of recorded biblical history, Satan has been trying to get mankind to doubt God and question His authority. Disguised as a serpent, Satan's first recorded words were, "Did God really say...?" (Genesis 3:1). God had warned that Adam and Eve were not to eat the fruit of a certain tree. Satan successfully tempted Eve away from God's authority—and she ate. As a result of Adam and Eve's disobedience and the entrance of sin into the world, mankind became separated from God. And up through today, Satan still uses the same tactic, trying to get people to doubt God.

Yet for all his power, Satan can be successfully thwarted. And when you firmly resist him, "he will flee from you" (James 4:7).

Satan attacks through weaknesses. Every person has weaknesses. For example, in Genesis 3, Eve's weakness was her pride. Satan implied that God was strict, stingy, and selfish for not wanting Eve to share God's knowledge. As the devil enticed Eve to eat the forbidden fruit, he said, "You will be like God, knowing good and evil" (Genesis 3:5).

Like Eve, we too fall into trouble when we dwell on the things we don't have, and accuse God of "holding out" on us. As a result we doubt God's wisdom and act on our own desires and are drawn into sin. Satan knows our weaknesses, and he will try to take advantage of them.

Satan's attacks can be resisted. Before Jesus began His public ministry, He "was led by the Spirit into the wilderness to be tempted by the devil" (Matthew 4:1). During that time of temptation, Jesus demonstrated to us how to withstand the devil. Satan's intention was to disqualify Jesus as man's only hope for redemption. It's worth noting that in these temptations, Satan focused on three areas in which people commonly struggle: (1) physical needs and desires, (2) possessions and power, and (3) pride.

With each temptation, Jesus countered from the Scriptures and did not give in to sin. Hebrews 4:15 says, "For we do not have a high priest who is unable to empathize with our weaknesses, but we have one who has been tempted in every way, just as we are—yet he did not sin." When you are tempted, Jesus knows firsthand what you are experiencing, and He is able to help you in your struggles. When you are tempted, lean on the power of the Holy Spirit and look to the instructions in God's Word with regard to what choices you are to make.

What Does This Mean for You?

The apostle Peter describes the devil as a vicious fighter, "a roaring lion looking for someone to devour" (1 Peter 5:8). The devil's goal is to disqualify you by getting you to succumb to temptation, fall into sin, and dishonor God. Although you as a Christian are assured of ultimate victory, for now, you must engage in the struggle until Christ returns.

Satan has had a lot of practice as a deceiver, beginning all the way back to the Garden of Eden. He and his demons are a supernatural force, and you need supernatural power to defeat them. Thankfully, God has not left you to battle by yourself. He has provided you with His Holy Spirit, His Word, and the spiritual armor described in Ephesians 6.

In warfare there is a saying: Know your enemy. How can you do that? Scripture tells you the tactics Satan uses and how to resist them. Rely on the power of the Holy Spirit, and follow the commands of Scripture. As Ephesians 6:10-11 says, "Be strong in the Lord and in the power of His might. Put on the whole armor of God, that you may be able to stand against the wiles of the devil" (NKJV).

17

Christians Are Perfect, and They Will Be!

Be perfect, therefore, as your heavenly Father is perfect
(Matthew 5:48).

By one sacrifice he has made perfect forever
those who are being made holy
(Hebrews 10:14).

Dear friends, now we are children of God, and
what we will be has not yet been made known. But
we know that when Christ appears, we shall
be like him, for we shall see him as he is
(1 John 3:2).

Wouldn't you agree that perfection should be the goal for every action, attitude, or endeavor you or I undertake? Doesn't the Bible tell us to do our best? Every effort should begin with perfection in mind. In ice skating or gymnastics competitions, the participants work hard in the hopes of receiving a perfect 10 rating. In baseball, the pitcher takes the mound in the hopes of striking out batters and throwing a no-hitter. Perfection is the standard in the physical realm.

In the spiritual realm, God, who is holy, has a standard as well—and it too is perfection! Jesus told a large crowd of people, "Be perfect, therefore, as your heavenly Father is perfect" (Matthew 5:48). Physical standards for perfection are not easily attained, but they are achievable. But when it comes to spiritual perfection, mankind cannot come anywhere close to God's standard of perfection. So what does all this have to do with the statement in the title of this chapter, "Christians are perfect, and they will be"? You may be thinking, *That sounds contradictory. How can this be?* Maybe I can explain it this way:

Perfection is modeled in Jesus. By definition, God must be a perfect being. So Jesus, as God in human flesh, was perfect and lived a life of perfection. Jesus' life then becomes the standard for living. Anything less than Jesus' perfection disqualifies a person from having an eternal relationship with a holy God. Given the fact we are spiritually fallen creatures, that sounds like a hopeless situation—a catch-22 scenario. God says you must be perfect to be with Him in heaven, but because of sin, you will never be perfect. This is where Jesus comes to our aid.

Perfection is offered in Jesus. Sin is what disqualifies all of mankind from achieving perfection in God's eyes. So it stands to reason that if your sin was removed, you would be perfect. That is why Jesus came to Earth—as the perfect man, Jesus, He was able to pay for your sin by His sacrificial death on the cross. Here's how the Bible states this amazing transaction: "God made [Jesus] who had no sin to be sin for us, so that in him we might become the righteousness of God" (2 Corinthians 5:21).

Perfection begins at salvation. When you accept Jesus as your Savior, God no longer sees you—rather, He sees Jesus and His righteousness. In God's eyes, you are perfect. Your sin has been taken care of by Jesus. You are a new person. As 2 Corinthians 5:17 says, "If anyone is in Christ, the new creation has come: The old has gone, the new is here!"

Through Christ's righteousness given to us at salvation, we

become perfect in God's eyes. That's why, when we die, we will immediately enter into heaven and the presence of our holy God. It's why Paul could declare, "We are confident, yes, well pleased rather to be absent from the body and to be present with the Lord" (2 Corinthians 5:8 NKJV). Theologians refer to this truth of perfection as our "position in Christ." We are perfect because we are forgiven. Our "perfect state" will not be official until we die and go to heaven, where we will be like Jesus—that is, perfect (1 John 3:2).

Perfection is not yet complete. As long as we who are Christians are alive on Earth, we will struggle with sin. Even though from a positional standpoint we are perfect, from a practical standpoint, our humanness still causes us to sin. But God has not left us to struggle on our own. The Holy Spirit indwells us to lead, guide, and instruct us and help us withstand the temptations that come our way.

God has started the process of perfection, and He will continue to perfect us until the day we die and the perfecting process is complete. As the apostle Paul said, "He who began a good work in you will carry it on to completion until the day of Christ Jesus" (Philippians 1:6).

Hebrews 10:14 explains both the practical and positional aspects of perfection: "By one sacrifice [Jesus] has made perfect forever [our position] those who are being made holy [our practice]."

Perfection is God at work in you. The Bible is clear about God's active involvement in our lives when it says, "It is God who is at work in you, both to will and to work for His good pleasure" (Philippians 2:13 NASB). God is moving us toward ultimate perfection. To assist in the process, He has provided moment-by-moment help. How is this done? Through the Holy Spirit. Jesus said, "The Helper, the Holy Spirit, whom the Father will send in My name, He will teach you all things, and bring to your remembrance all things that I said to you" (John 14:26).

Perfection is a goal toward which to strive. When you arrive in heaven, your perfection will be complete. But until then, you are to aspire to be as much like Jesus as possible. In what areas of your life can you do this?

> —Character. Character is a matter of the heart. The Bible says, "Above all else, guard your heart, for everything you do flows from it" (Proverbs 4:23). Since your actions and attitudes are determined by your heart, make sure your heart lines up with the standards God sets in His Word. Then you'll show right character.

> —Holiness. This world is not your home. You are only passing through on your way to dwell with God. Your citizenship is in heaven (Philippians 3:20). Therefore, you are to separate yourself from the world's sinful values. Choose the things of God rather than the things of this world.

> —Maturity. Just as physical strength is not achieved all at once, so spiritual strength—maturity—is also not achieved quickly. Such growth comes in stages. It's like the different behaviors you can expect from a person who is growing up—a baby, a child, a teenager, then an adult. God also expects you to be growing in spiritual maturity, and with that growth, He expects different behavior from you.

What Does This Mean for You?

If you are a believer, perfection is a future reality for you. However, because of the sin that dwells in your human flesh, perfection is not possible in the present. Nevertheless, your disposition to sin must not keep you from striving to grow more Christlike. Christ calls you to excel, to rise above mediocrity, and to mature spiritually while looking forward to that time when perfection will no longer be the goal, but the reality.

When will that time be? The apostle John stated it this way:

"Dear friends, now we are children of God, and what we will be has not yet been made known. But we know that when Christ appears, we shall be like him, for we shall see him as he is" (1 John 3:2). Today you are perfect because you are *in* Christ. But one day you will be perfect because you will be *with* Christ!

18

It's Not About What You Do, but About What Christ Did

Jesus answered, "I am the way and the truth and the life. No one comes to the Father except through me"
(John 14:6).

Salvation is found in no one else, for there is no other name [Jesus Christ] under heaven given to mankind by which we must be saved
(Acts 4:12).

God made him who had no sin to be sin for us, so that in him we might become the righteousness of God
(2 Corinthians 5:21).

Do you know how many religions there are in the world? At first glance, it may seem like there are hundreds, if not thousands. But in reality, there are only two—God's and man's. Man's religion, no matter what name it goes by, will always be built on a foundation of self-righteousness. Man's religion asks the question, What must I do to earn immortality? Man's religion is built on the merit system—religious effort that earns eternal life.

God's religion, as revealed in the Bible, rests upon the foundation of God's righteousness and the atoning sacrifice of God's Son,

Jesus Christ. God says, "You cannot do anything to merit heaven. I have already done everything necessary by sending My Son, Jesus Christ, to die on the cross so you may live." Simply put, salvation is not based on what you can do, but on what Christ has done. And what has He done? Theologians refer to Christ's accomplishment as "the atonement"—that is, a covering, a payment, or a sacrifice.

Christ's actions were preplanned. God is eternal, and therefore His actions are eternal. Everything from the creation of the universe to the entrance of sin into the world; to the birth, life, death, and resurrection of Jesus, the eternal Son; to what will happen in the last days was determined in eternity. In God's plan, Jesus would be the means of reconciling sinful mankind to Himself. The apostle Peter wrote, "You were redeemed...with the precious blood of Christ, a lamb without blemish or defect. He was chosen before the creation of the world" (1 Peter 1:18-20).

Christ became a man. In eternity past, God in three co-equal persons of the Father, Son, and Holy Spirit determined that the eternal Son become a man and live a holy life. He would ultimately satisfy a holy God's requirement for the payment of sin. God's righteousness would then be satisfied, and a holy God could once again have a personal relationship with man.

Christ had to die. One element of worship in the Old Testament was animal sacrifices, which were continually offered up to God for the sins of the people of Israel. It was through the shedding of the blood that atonement was offered (Leviticus 17:11). These sacrifices were needed on a ongoing basis because the people continued to sin.

But these sacrifices could only *cover* the people's sin—not *take away* their sin. It was only through the death of Jesus, who was sinless, that the ultimate sacrifice was made that would satisfy, once and for all, the righteous demands of a holy God. The writer of Hebrews states it this way: "We have been made holy through the sacrifice of the body of Jesus Christ once for all" (Hebrews 10:10).

Christ's death was as a substitute. Ever since Adam and Eve sinned in the Garden of Eden, man has been in rebellion against a holy God. And the punishment for sin is death. But rather than let man die for his own sin, God provided a substitute. Who better to pay for the sins of the whole world than the perfect man—Jesus, who "committed no sin, and no deceit was found in his mouth" (1 Peter 2:22)! Jesus took our place on the cross. He became a substitute for us: "God made him who had no sin to be sin for us, so that in him we might become the righteousness of God" (2 Corinthians 5:21).

Christ's death secured forgiveness. In the Old Testament sacrificial system, sacrifices for sin were made constantly. But those sacrifices provided only a temporary covering. God's justice was not satisfied until Jesus' own blood was shed on the cross. It was His sacrifice that procured complete forgiveness.

As a result, there is no longer any need for priests to offer additional sacrifices. As the Bible says in Hebrews 7:27, "Unlike the other high priests, he does not need to offer sacrifices day after day, first for his own sins, and then for the sins of the people. He sacrificed for their sins once for all when he offered himself." Christ's death secured forgiveness—once for all!

Christ's death must be applied. At the beginning of this chapter we established that ultimately, there are only two religions in the world: man's religion of good works, or God's religion of Christ's work done on the cross. If you choose to depend on your works, you will be choosing poorly because the Bible says salvation is "not by works of righteousness" (Titus 3:5 NKJV). No amount of righteous deeds and good works can help you get to heaven. God's grace is your only hope—"the gift of God is eternal life in Christ Jesus our Lord" (Romans 6:23).

Grace is God's voluntary and loving favor given to those whom He chooses to save. You cannot earn God's grace, nor do you deserve it. Without God's grace, no person can be saved. To receive it, you must acknowledge that you cannot save yourself, that only God can save you, and that it's possible only by faith in Christ, as defined in Scripture: "It is by grace you have been saved, through faith—and this is not from yourselves, it is the gift of God—not by works, so that no one can boast" (Ephesians 2:8-9).

What Does This Mean for You?

It must be extremely unsettling for people who are trying to work their way to heaven to never know if they have done enough—if they are going to make it. You might be one of these people. Are you doing enough to merit eternal life? How will you know when and if you have satisfied God's requirements? Can you trust your eternal destiny to a human estimation of your worthiness?

By contrast, how liberating it is to know that you cannot do anything to earn your salvation. Your salvation was purchased at the greatest of all prices—the death of Jesus. As a result of His payment for your sin, the Father offers you the gift of eternal life, which must be received by faith, not earned by works.

If you, by God's grace alone, have received this greatest of all gifts, you should be constantly praising God "because of the surpassing grace [He] has given you. Thanks be to God for his indescribable gift!" (2 Corinthians 9:14-15).

Furthermore, with continued gratitude for this free gift, you should be telling others about God's offer of grace. What a deal—a free gift! Be faithful to spread this good news to anyone who will listen.

And finally, because of God's grace, you should actively seek to help and serve others with kindness, charity, and goodness. These actions do not earn salvation—they are simply the fruit that comes from being made a new person in Christ.

19

Even When It May Not Seem Like It, God Really Is in Control

The king's heart is in the hand of the LORD, like the rivers of water; He turns it wherever He wishes (Proverbs 21:1 NKJV).

Those God foreknew he also predestined to be conformed to the image of his Son, that he might be the firstborn among many brothers and sisters. And those he predestined, he also called; those he called, he also justified; those he justified, he also glorified (Romans 8:29-30).

Who has known the mind of the Lord? Or who has been his counselor? (Romans 11:34).

All through life—when you were young, and now as an adult—you've been subject to the authority of others, whether in your home, at school, or at work. I am guessing that, for the most part, you have not had any problems with doing what people in authority over you have asked you to do. That's because you've recognized that the person who was in charge—whether it was a parent, a teacher, or a boss—had the final say.

Yet while many of us don't have much of a problem with following human authority, we find it a bit harder to yield to God's authority. Why is that? He is after all, the Creator and Lord of all things, and consequently is free to do whatever He wills. He is not subject to nor answerable to anyone. As created beings, we are in no position to judge God for what He does. One phrase theologians use to speak of God's authority is "the sovereignty of God." Let's see what the Bible says about God's sovereignty:

God's sovereignty is beyond comprehension. Job said, "How great is God—beyond our understanding!" (Job 36:26). Nothing can compare to God. His power and presence are awesome, and when He speaks to us today from His Word, we must listen. Unfortunately, sometimes we think we have a better idea of how we should live our lives and make our decisions. Because we can't understand something God is asking of us, we want to question or argue or rebel. In Romans 9, Paul used an interesting illustration to explain God's authority over us: "Does not the potter have the right to make out of the same lump of clay some pottery for special purposes and some for common use?" (verse 21).

God's sovereignty is eternal. In eternity past, before time began, God selected certain individuals to have a special relationship with Him. As 2 Timothy 1:9 says, God "saved us and called us with a holy calling, not according to our works, but according to His own purpose and grace which was given to us in Christ Jesus before time began" (NKJV). This act of salvation, along with all other actions God would take, was determined in eternity past, waiting to be accomplished in time.

God's sovereignty confronts free will. Some see a contradiction between divine sovereignty and free will, the latter of which is an often misunderstood term. Man's will is free in that he makes willing choices that have actual consequences. Yet man's will is not morally neutral; rather, it is in bondage to sin and, without divine grace, he chooses freely and consistently to reject God (Romans 3:10-11; Ephesians 2:1-3; 2 Timothy 2:25-26).

Scripture affirms both divine sovereignty and man's willing

activity. For instance, when Pharaoh confronted Moses, Pharaoh acted entirely in accordance with his own will. Yet God says, "I have raised you up for this very purpose, that I might show you my power" (Exodus 9:16). Likewise, the crucifixion of Christ was carried out by sinful men, and at the same time was permitted by the purpose of God (Acts 2:23; 4:27-28).

Even a person's salvation is determined by God's sovereign intervention. Acts 13:48 declares, "All who were appointed for eternal life believed," and Acts 16:14 says of Lydia, "She was a worshiper of God. The Lord opened her heart to respond to Paul's message" of salvation.

God's sovereignty affirms evangelism. Many Christians use God's sovereignty as an excuse to not share about Christ with unbelievers. They reason, "If God has already 'elected' certain people to salvation, why do I need to speak up or pray...or talk to non-Christians about Christ?" Yet in Matthew 11:25-30, Jesus affirmed the absolute sovereignty of God and at the same time invited sinners to Himself for salvation.

Paul too began his extensive treatment of divine sovereignty by expressing his burden for his lost kinsmen (Romans 9:1-5). Yet he also expressed his heartfelt prayer for their salvation (Romans 10:1) and said, "Everyone who calls on the name of the Lord will be saved" (Romans 10:13). So even though God is sovereign, we are to be active in reaching out to the lost and inviting them to salvation in Christ.

God's sovereignty still holds mankind responsible. How can God be sovereign and hold man responsible for his actions? The relationship between these two concepts is mysterious but not contradictory. The Bible teaches that man is accountable to God for his actions—as Paul said, "God will repay each person according to what they have done" (Romans 2:6).

Paul addressed the tension between man's accountability and God's sovereignty, and simply affirmed both (Romans 9:19-29). This is one of many seeming contradictions that our finite minds cannot resolve; therefore, we can only fall back on scriptures like

Deuteronomy 29:29, which states: "The secret things belong to the LORD our God, but the things revealed belong to us and to our children forever, that we may follow all the words of this law."

God's sovereignty doesn't need to be explained. God is not required to explain anything to us. He made this clear to Job, who felt God owed him answers for the many bad things that had happened in his life. Finally, as if God had had enough, "the LORD spoke to Job out of the storm" (Job 38:1). Over the next four chapters, God reminded Job of just how little he knew. If Job didn't fully understand the workings of God's physical creation, which he could see, then how could he possibly understand God's mind and character, which he could not see? There is no standard or criterion higher than God Himself by which to judge.

What Does This Mean for You?

The world seems to be out of control. Sin and evil are rampant. This makes it easy to think God doesn't care about what's going on, or that He isn't capable of dealing with it.

But God does care, and He is capable of doing whatever He wants—but in His timing. This trust is well-founded because that's exactly what God told Moses with regard to the Israelites when they were held captive in Egypt:

> *I have seen* the misery of my people in Egypt...
>
> *I am concerned* about their suffering.
>
> So *I have come down* to rescue them...
>
> *I am sending you* to Pharaoh (Exodus 3:7-10).

This is the same sovereign God who today sees us, is concerned about us, has sent His Son to die for our sins, and will return one day to deal with evil. The Bible tells us all these things, and you can trust what it says. Even when it may not seem like it, God really is in control. Your response should be to willingly submit to His authority and rest in His care.

20

You Cannot Escape from God's Presence

Go and make disciples of all nations...And surely I
am with you always, to the very end of the age
(Matthew 28:19-20).

I give them eternal life, and they shall never perish;
no one will snatch them out of my hand. My Father,
who has given them to me, is greater than all; no
one can snatch them out of my Father's hand
(John 10:28-29).

My prayer is not that you take them out of the world
but that you protect them from the evil one
(John 17:15).

I am an only child, which had some great benefits for me while I was growing up. I didn't have to share my toys or bike with any brothers or sisters. I didn't have to share my parents' affection with other siblings. I was very much the center of attention. But there was one persistent problem—I didn't have anyone to play with at home! So I was always trying to make friends and find playmates. Even though I had my parents, I still craved to be with other kids my age. In that sense, I didn't want to be alone.

Very few people in this world like to be alone. And that's how it should be! God said, "It is not good for the man to be alone" (Genesis 2:18), so God created woman as a companion. God originally intended this companionable relationship to exist between a husband and wife. But God also could have been speaking about His desire to have a presence in the life of His people. That's exactly what Jesus was promising when He said, "Surely I am with you always, to the very end of the age" (Matthew 28:20).

God's presence is real. Perhaps while in a reflective mood, the psalmist asked the question, "Where can I go from Your Spirit? Where can I flee from your presence?" (Psalm 139:7). He then listed all the places he might go, but he would never be able to escape God's knowledge or presence. Even in the highest, deepest, farthest places, God would still be with him. Elsewhere he said, "Even though I walk through the darkest valley, I will fear no evil, for you are with me" (Psalm 23:4).

God's presence is personal. One of God's characteristics is that He is in all places at the same time. This means He is *omnipresent.* In the Old Testament, God was personally present in the lives of key individuals like Joshua, who became leader of the children of Israel after Moses died. God said, "Do not be afraid; do not be discouraged, for the LORD your God will be with you wherever you go" (Joshua 1:9). God's presence was with Joshua because Joshua had an important mission to perform—leading the children of Israel into the Promised Land.

In the New Testament, with the arrival of the Holy Spirit, God is present in those who are believers in Jesus Christ. God is everywhere present, but He is personally present and will be present with each Christian for as long as he or she lives on this Earth. Then at the moment of death, that believer will be immediately transported into God's presence in heaven. There will be no delays. God is present with His children here on Earth, and they will be in His presence in heaven. What a powerful and comforting promise and prospect!

God's presence is a good thing. Sadly, God's presence is not the primary passion of many Christians. Rather than spending their time living and basking in God's presence moment by moment, they are like Adam and Eve (I'm sure you know the story!). At one point Adam and Eve walked with God continuously, but when they sinned, they "hid themselves from the presence of the LORD God among the trees of the garden" (Genesis 3:8 NKJV). Their sin altered the relationship they had enjoyed with God. As a result, they tried to hide from Him.

If you're not all that excited about living in God's presence, then check for sin in your life. Confess it to God. Do your part to close the gap between you and the Lord. And revel once again in the truth that God's presence in your life is a good thing—the best thing!

God's presence is a comfort. If you are like me (and probably everyone else!), you often wish you could avoid pain, grief, loss, sorrow, failure, and a host of other difficulties. You even wish you could rid your life of those small yet daily frustrations that constantly wear you down. But note how God's presence comes to your aid in times of trouble:

> The righteous cry out, and the LORD hears them;
> he delivers them from all their troubles.
> The LORD is close to the brokenhearted
> and saves those who are crushed in spirit
> (Psalm 34:17-18).

Did you catch all that? God promises to be a source of power, courage, and strength and to help the righteous through their problems. Sometimes He chooses to deliver us from our problems. But it's exciting when He chooses to give us the strength to endure through them, for it is then that we are especially reminded His presence is with us!

When difficulties strike (and strike they will!), don't get upset and frustrated with God. Don't have a panic attack. Instead, remember that God is present with you. Acknowledge that you need Him at your side. Cry out to Him, run to Him, cling to Him. Count on His presence. No matter how bad your trials are, the Lord is with you. He is always with His children.

What Does This Mean for You?

It's amazing to realize that God is present with you at all times. What, then, is an appropriate response? You should share this fact with anyone who will listen. You should talk about God when you are with others, especially unbelievers. Talk about the reality of God's presence in your life. Verbally lift up your thanks to God at mealtime for His faithfulness to you.

Unbelievers cannot see God, but they can see Him in your life. Fellow believers can see Him in you as well. Make it a point to insert His name into your conversations. Refer to Him often. When others are discouraged or need a faith boost, speak of the Lord's presence.

Here are some ways you can practice the presence of God. When you receive a paycheck, before opening it, thank God for His provision. When you receive a letter or get a phone call from someone with a problem, pray with him and together share his issue or concern with God. When you get into a car or on an airplane, pray. When you eat, pray. When you're sad, pray...glad, pray...fearful, pray...in need, pray.

This chapter is not about prayer, so why do you pray? Because you believe God is present with you at all times. Your every breath is a reminder of God's presence. God is in your every circumstance, "for the LORD your God will be with you wherever you go" (Joshua 1:9).

21

Nothing Can Separate You from God's Love

This is the will of him who sent me, that I shall lose none of all those he has given me, but raise them up at the last day (John 6:39).

Who shall separate us from the love of Christ? Shall trouble or hardship or persecution or famine or nakedness or danger or sword?...No, in all these things we are more than conquerors through him who loved us (Romans 8:35-37).

When you believed, you were marked in him with a seal, the promised Holy Spirit, who is a deposit guaranteeing our inheritance until the redemption of those who are God's possession—to the praise of his glory (Ephesians 1:13-14).

Do you love to start projects, hobbies, or ministries? That has been true about me for years. And it's been a great joy to see many of my ventures come to pass and continue on. But here's a confession: I also have a tendency to leave some of my projects unfinished (I have a storage unit to prove my point!).

Starting something new is thrilling, especially when you have lots of ideas. But sometimes after we get started on one venture it's easy to get distracted by yet another one…and then, before we know it, we are off and running with our latest inspiration!

That's when I realize how fortunate I am to have others who come alongside to help me finish what I've started. These wonderful friends are at the top of my "thanksgiving" list to God as committed finishers. But most of all, I—and you too—should be thanking God that when it comes to our eternal destiny, God is both a starter and a finisher! Every believer is one of God's works in progress, and God always finishes what He starts. Let's look at the specifics:

God's work started in eternity. According to 2 Timothy 1:9, God's work in your life started in eternity, when He determined, by His grace, to redeem you to Himself: "He has saved us and called us to a holy life—not because of anything we have done but because of his own purpose and grace. This grace was given us in Christ Jesus before the beginning of time." God's work continued on in time as He sent His Son, the sinless Lord Jesus Christ, to die for sinners—which includes you and me. Then on the day when you placed your trust in Christ, salvation took root, and God began His good work in you.

God's work will be completed. Mark it well: When God starts a project, He will complete it. God has given you this promise in Philippians 1:6:

> He who began a good work in you will carry it on
> to completion until the day of Christ Jesus.

God has promised that He will help each person who embraces His Son as Savior to grow in His grace until they are complete—yes, complete! Nothing can separate us from God and His promise to keep us secure until we enter heaven.

From the time you experienced the "new birth" of salvation (John 3:7), God has been at work in you. And He will continue to carry on His work until you see your Lord face-to-face (1 John

3:2). No matter what happens along the way, God's work in you cannot be stopped.

God's work is secure. God is *sovereign.* This term is used to speak of a king or ruler who has complete power. That is an accurate description of God. No one has more power than God. He alone created and maintains this universe. Nothing has happened, can happen, or will happen that overrules His power.

The apostle Paul described how secure you are in God's love when he wrote, "I am convinced that neither death nor life, neither angels nor demons, neither the present nor the future, nor any powers, neither height nor depth, nor anything else in all creation, will be able to separate us from the love of God that is in Christ Jesus our Lord" (Romans 8:38-39).

You can be confident that God's power and love are strong enough to keep you spiritually secure to the end, to completion.

God's work is internal. God's work in your life did not stop at salvation. No, that was just the beginning. God has given you His Holy Spirit to work in you. Jesus said, "I will ask the Father, and he will give you another advocate to help you and be with you forever—the Spirit of truth…for he lives with you and will be in you" (John 14:16-17).

Can you imagine? The Holy Spirit comes to live in you when you accept Jesus as your Savior. And Jesus did not qualify that residence. He said the Holy Spirit will "be with you forever." God has given you an "advocate," a helper, a resident tutor to enable you to be more like Jesus every day and to guide you into all truth (John 16:13). As long as you are alive, the Holy Spirit will continue His work in you and never leave you.

What Does This Mean for You?

Do you have a high view of God? The Bible says He is in control of all things—and that includes your salvation. Jesus Christ sacrificed Himself to save you, and now He lives to intercede for you (Hebrews 7:25). His care and concern will carry you until you meet Jesus face-to-face—in heaven. That's the finish line! God will ensure that you cross the finish line, complete and perfect in Him.

All of this means you can live your life without any doubts or fears. Nothing and no one can separate you from God's love and the completion of the work He has started in you. With that in mind, here is what He asks of you:

Be encouraged. Take heart that God is not finished with you. You are a work in progress. And as an unfinished project, you have room for growth. Whatever obstacle, failure, or speed bump comes your way, know that God is using those challenges to perfect and complete what He has begun in you. God is working for your good and His glory.

Be growing spiritually. How? Here's the short list: Confess your sin. Obey God's Word. Walk by the Spirit. Grow in grace and knowledge. Enlist the help of others. Worship with God's people. Evaluate your progress. Give thanks always.

Be confident. Because God has promised that you are secure in Him, you can be confident that your eternal destiny is absolutely certain. God, who loves you unconditionally, does not leave anything to chance. He will ensure that what He has started in your life will be completed.

> To him who is able to keep you from stumbling and
> to present you before his glorious presence
> without fault and with great joy—
> to the only God our Savior be glory, majesty,
> power and authority, through Jesus Christ our Lord,
> before all ages, now and forevermore! Amen (Jude 24-25).

22

Sin Has Consequences, Both Now and Eternally

*All have sinned and fall short of the glory of God
(Romans 3:23).*

*Sin entered the world through one man, and
death through sin, and in this way death
came to all people, because all sinned
(Romans 5:12).*

*The wages of sin is death
(Romans 6:23).*

Many people, when they hear the words *sin* or *sinner*, immediately think of someone like the 1960s film character Elmer Gantry, a con man who went around small-town America during the Depression era "selling" religion. The topic of sin and its consequences is not a popular subject, and those who insist on talking about it are not invited to many parties. But this is as it's always been. Jesus confronted the religious leaders of His day with their sin, and was crucified. Even though sin is not a pleasant subject to talk about, we must address it if we want to become right with God and spend eternity with Him in heaven.

Sin is falling short of God's standard. During the early days of the formation of the nation of Israel, God repeatedly had to remind the people, including Moses and the leaders, that "I am the LORD your God. You shall therefore consecrate yourselves, and you shall be holy; for I am holy" (Leviticus 11:44 NKJV). Jesus clarified God's standard of holiness when He declared, "You shall be perfect, just as your Father in heaven is perfect" (Matthew 5:48 NKJV). It stands to reason that a holy God can accept nothing less than holy people: The standard is perfection. Every action that violates God's standards is defined as sin. Very simply, sin is missing God's mark of perfection. There are no shades of sin. Every person on the face of the Earth must live a perfect life if they want to enjoy eternal life and be with God when they die. Only one man, Jesus Christ, has fulfilled this requirement.

Sin is not temptation. Or put another way, temptation is not sin. Disguised as a serpent, Satan tempted Eve to disobey God. Eve gave in to the temptation and ate the forbidden fruit, and therefore sinned. Satan continues to tempt people by feeding on their natural desires and attacking their areas of greatest weakness. Temptation is usually subtle and offers what may seem like a harmless choice, as Eve observed: "The woman saw that the fruit of the tree was good for food and pleasing to the eye, and also desirable for gaining wisdom" (Genesis 3:6). Unless temptation is checked, it can lead to sin (just ask Adam and Eve!). Again, the only man who has ever lived without sin is Jesus. He is the only one who has ever lived up to God's standard of perfection.

Sin has its consequences. God's "eyes are too pure to look on evil; [He] cannot tolerate wrongdoing" (Habakkuk 1:13). So what are the consequences of sin for one who fails to live a perfectly holy life, or falls short of the glory of God (Romans 3:23)? Adam and Eve learned through painful experience about sin's consequences.

> Alienation—As soon as Adam and Eve sinned, they
> hid from God. They experienced shame, guilt, fear,
> and self-vindication. Adam blamed Eve, and Eve
> blamed the serpent. Sin had broken their close rela-
> tionship with God.

Judgment—God warned this first couple that if they ate from a certain tree they would die. Their death came in two phases. First, they experienced spiritual death as they became alienated from God. Second, they would eventually experience physical death. God's judgment also included the woman's sorrow in childbirth, and the man's sorrow in tilling the soil to provide food for his family. Adam's sorrow would be multiplied because of God's curse upon the ground, which would produce thorns and thistles.

Separation—God, who is holy, drove Adam and Eve out of the Garden of Eden because of their sin. They could no longer have a personal and visible relationship with Him. This separation was as much an act of mercy as it was punishment. If these two sinners—Adam and Eve—were to have eaten of *the tree of life* (Genesis 3:22-23), they would have lived forever in a state of death and alienation with no chance of redemption. But God had a plan. He promised to send a Savior (verse 15) who would defeat Satan and restore the relationship between mankind and God.

Damnation—Sin has doomed mankind. It is a fatal disease that affects all of us and will eventually kill us. Why? Because God's penalty for sin is death—as Romans 6:23 says, "The wages of sin is death." Death comes in two stages. *Spiritual death* took place when Adam and Eve sinned. As descendants of Adam and Eve, we are also dead in our trespasses and sin (Ephesians 2:1). *Physical death* will eventually overtake every living person. Unless spiritual death is reversed, it becomes permanent upon physical death. In other words, those who do not receive Christ's sinless death as a payment for their sin will not only experience spiritual death, but also eternal death. This is the ultimate consequence of sin and is referred to as "the second death" in Revelation 21:8. This second death will separate unrepentant sinners from the presence of God for all eternity.

Repercussions—The lie of Satan is that sin is an individual act that affects only the person who commits it. We know that's not the case because Adam and Eve's sin ended up having deadly consequences on every single human born since! King David is another example of the repercussions of sin: His sin of adultery with Bathsheba not only affected Bathsheba, but also resulted in the death of Uriah, her husband. Then the child who was conceived as a result of their illicit affair died. And the consequences didn't stop there. For the next 20 years, David's household would experience strife and even treason. No, sin is never committed in a vacuum. Other people will always be sucked into your sin and suffer consequences.

Sin's only cure—To repeat, sin is a fatal disease! Unless God steps into our lives, we will succumb to the ultimate consequence of sin—eternal death. With Jesus' death and resurrection, God has offered a solution to sin and death. When Jesus said, "It is finished" (John 19:30), His death "paid in full" the penalty for sin. His perfect sacrifice made it unnecessary to continue Old Testament sacrifices. Sin and death have been vanquished in Jesus—"for the wages of sin is death, but the gift of God is eternal life in Christ Jesus our Lord" (Romans 6:23). Those who accept what Jesus has done on their behalf can live eternally with God and escape the ultimate consequence of sin.

What Does This Means for You?

Sin's consequences have been dealt with in Jesus, but sin still wages war in your mortal body (Romans 7:18). In Jesus, God has forgiven your sins and they can no longer condemn you, but you'll still struggle with sin and feel its consequences. When you allow sin into your life, it will affect your relationship with God and others. When you confess your sin, it does not affect your salvation—that was forever settled by Jesus. Confession restores your relationship with God. The battle is fierce, but your victory is assured: "There is now no condemnation for those who are in Christ Jesus" (Romans 8:1).

23

God Has a Wonderful Purpose for Your Life

Before I formed you in the womb I knew
you, before you were born I set you apart; I
appointed you as a prophet to the nations
(Jeremiah 1:5).

The Lord said to Ananias, "Go! This man is my chosen
instrument to proclaim my name to the Gentiles
and their kings and to the people of Israel"
(Acts 9:15-16).

Now when David had served God's purpose
in his own generation, he fell asleep
(Acts 13:36).

Viktor Frankl was an Austrian psychiatrist who worked as a slave laborer in an incredibly brutal German concentration camp during World War II. During that time, Frankl noticed that some of the prisoners collapsed under the pressure of the harsh demands, gave up, and died, while others continued to stay alive. What made the difference?

Using his medical training, Dr. Frankl talked to the surviving inmates. Over the months, he noticed a pattern. Those prisoners who had something to live for—an objective that gave a sense of meaning to their lives or a purpose—were the ones who seemed to be able to mobilize their inner strength and survive.

Each survivor had a focus and a passion that kept them alive. And Frankl was no exception. He had begun writing a book and possessed a fierce desire to survive and finish it. After the war, Frankl completed what had motivated him to stay alive—his book.

Frankl's experience illustrates for us the power of purpose. There is nothing as potent as a life lived with passion and purpose. But what if you had a purpose that wasn't merely inspired by your own desires? What if you had a purpose that originated from a higher source—a divine source—from God Himself? Wouldn't that be a grand purpose indeed? Truly one of the most important teachings in the Bible is that God has a wonderful purpose for your life.

God's purpose gives true meaning to your life. Dr. Frankl's observations in the war camp were right on—having a purpose gives meaning to life. But even a life purpose, as potent as it is, makes little sense if it has significance only in this life. For once your life is over, all that is left is a memory—and your purpose has ended with your death.

But that's not the case if you are a believer in Christ. Why? Because you have a purpose that does not cease with death. Yours is a purpose that was determined in eternity past, a purpose that is being realized now during your lifetime and will be finalized in eternity future.

Understanding you have a purpose given to you by God should fill your life with meaning and significance. It helps you realize that all that happens to you is for a reason—it's part of God's plans for you, as Romans 8:28 states: "We know that in all things God works for the good of those who love him, who have been called according to his purpose."

Your life will take on its intended meaning when you grasp God's purpose. Those Christians in the past who have understood God's purpose for them have lived bold and courageous lives because they knew exactly what God's will was for them. And the same can be true for you.

God's purpose is unique for you. Has it registered yet? You are singularly special to God! God has sovereignly prepared you for a purpose that is unique only to you and allows for your own unique contributions to His work here on Earth.

God had a life purpose for David (Acts 13:36). Even though David faltered at times, he followed God's purpose for his life—and he fulfilled it. His heart for God allowed him to be used mightily by God in his own generation in spite of his shortcomings. Similarly, in the New Testament, we read that the apostle Paul was given the task of taking the gospel to the Gentiles (Acts 9:15-16). As he committed himself to doing this, he fulfilled God's purpose for him.

Like David and Paul, you too have a purpose God desires for you to fulfill. You have been given a unique set of spiritual gifts (1 Corinthians 12:4-11), a unique personality, and unique life experiences, all to be used in unique ways by God. Realizing that God has a specific purpose for you should keep you from ever feeling discouraged, inadequate, or insignificant.

God's purpose requires patience. When the Old Testament prophet Jeremiah was a young adult, he received a message from God: "Before I formed you in the womb I knew you, before you were born I set you apart; I appointed you as a prophet to the nations" (Jeremiah 1:5). Bible scholars estimate Jeremiah was between 20 to 30 years old when God said this. If that is true, then Jeremiah lived two to three decades in a tiny village without knowing about the grand purpose God had for him.

Like Jeremiah, you may need to wait patiently before God reveals His purpose for you. As you wait, do as Jeremiah did, and be faithful in whatever situation you are in right now. As you wait on the Lord, commit yourself to following Him, growing spiritually mature, and serving others in whatever ways you can.

God's purpose requires obedience. Discovering and fulfilling God's purpose for your life begins with obedience—that is what prepared

Jeremiah for use by God. If you read the book of Jeremiah, you will discover that very few people—if any—desired to serve God in that time. Jeremiah was one person God could use because he had not disqualified himself through disobedience. He was qualified to serve God because of his faithful, daily obedience.

Remember, God's purpose for your life is realized more and more with your every act of obedience. Obedience is God's starting point for you when it comes to understanding His purpose. Then stand back and behold as God reveals the next step in your future and His will for you!

God has a common purpose for all believers. Are you still wondering, *What is my purpose?* Well, be encouraged. As with Jeremiah and the apostle Paul, your purpose will have a unique nature to it. But there is also a sense in which all believers share common purposes. Listed below are some of the common purposes that God asks of every believer:

> come to repentance (2 Peter 3:9)
>
> be conformed to the image of His Son (Romans 8:29)
>
> glorify God (1 Corinthians 6:20 NKJV)
>
> love and respect your spouse (Ephesians 5:22-33)
>
> care for and spiritually train your children (Ephesians 6:4)
>
> keep yourself pure (1 Thessalonians 4:4)
>
> be His witness (Acts 1:8)

What Does This Mean for You?

Like David, Jeremiah, and the apostle Paul, you have a purpose—God's purpose. God has planned to work through you in ways that no one else can fulfill. Are you committed to doing what God desires of you as a Christian? Have you set goals, or made yourself available to minister to others? Setting goals and making commitments will put you on the path to being purposeful. If you haven't yet, start setting goals for how you can personally and positively affect those closest to you. As you are faithful to carry out your ministry, God will continue to unfold His purpose for you in the days ahead. Put another way, your faithfulness to God's purpose *today* will guide you into God's purpose for *tomorrow*.

24

In the Spiritual Life, No Pain, No Gain

Let us purify ourselves from everything that contaminates body and spirit, perfecting holiness out of reverence for God (2 Corinthians 7:1).

When Christ, who is your life, appears, then you also will appear with him in glory. Put to death, therefore, whatever belongs to your earthly nature: sexual immorality, impurity, lust, evil desires and greed, which is idolatry (Colossians 3:4–5).

Make every effort to add to your faith goodness; and to goodness, knowledge; and to knowledge, self-control; and to self-control, perseverance; and to perseverance, godliness; and to godliness, mutual affection; and to mutual affection, love. For if you possess these qualities in increasing measure, they will keep you from being ineffective and unproductive in your knowledge of our Lord Jesus Christ (2 Peter 1:5–8).

In the Old Testament, God expressed the desire that the children of Israel be a holy people. He told them, "Be holy, because I am holy" (Leviticus 11:44). A key reason for this command is that He knew the people of Israel would be exposed to and surrounded by other nations that worshipped false gods, and He didn't want His people to be tempted to turn to idolatry.

To help prepare the Israelites to withstand these errant influences, God gave them laws with instructions about clothing, diet, and a general prohibition against social interaction with pagan nations. God's people were to make a committed effort to separate themselves from the nations around them and remain holy.

God's desire for His people to be holy did not change with the coming of the Messiah, Jesus Christ. His call to holiness and separation is a consistent theme in the New Testament, which makes it an important teaching for all believers today. Theologians refer to the process of growing in holiness as *sanctification,* which refers simply to spiritual growth.

There are two aspects to a believer's sanctification. First, every believer, from the moment of conversion, is a new person and is given what is called *positional sanctification.* In God's eyes, because of Christ's work on the cross, a believer has a perfect standing of holiness. Believers are "sanctified in Christ" (1 Corinthians 1:2). This type of sanctification is a product of God's grace alone, and no effort is required on our part.

Then there is also what's known as *progressive sanctification.* When we commit ourselves to living holy, we become in practice what we are in position. While Christ's righteousness has already been given to us, still, we need to live out that righteousness by making right decisions, right choices, and living as God wants us to live. Because we live in a sin-filled world and we are frequently tempted by sinful desires, spiritual growth is always a challenge. That is why we can say, "In the spiritual life, no pain, no gain." It takes diligence and effort to grow more and more like Christ and be set apart for God's use.

What else do we need to know about progressive sanctification, or spiritual growth?

Spiritual growth is ongoing. Even though we will never be free from sin in this life, God still commands us to make an effort to deal with sin. This is what Paul meant when he instructed believers to "continue to work out your salvation with fear and trembling, for it is God who works in you to will and to act in order to fulfill his good purpose" (Philippians 2:12-13). To "work out your salvation" means to do what is necessary to be "set apart" as a child of God.

Spiritual growth requires self-denial. Jesus said, "Whoever wants to be my disciple must deny themselves and take up their cross and follow me" (Matthew 16:24). Being Christ's disciples requires sacrifice—it requires saying no to the pleasures of the world.

Spiritual growth requires discipline. When the apostle Paul taught about spiritual growth, he used the illustration of a runner who goes all out to win. His point was that the Christian life requires hard work, self-denial, and grueling preparation. As Christians, we are running toward our heavenly reward. This race requires that we be diligent. Our spiritual progress depends upon it. Paul exhorted, "Run in such a way as to get the prize. Everyone who competes in the games goes into strict training. They do it to get a crown that will not last, but we do it to get a crown that will last forever" (1 Corinthians 9:25).

Spiritual growth requires obeying God's Word. When Jesus prayed for the disciples, He asked the Father, "Sanctify them by the truth; your word is truth" (John 17:17). That is, God's Word is able to sanctify us. As we read it, study it, listen to it preached, and with the help of the Holy Spirit apply its truths to our lives, we grow and become more and more like Christ. Spiritual growth is accomplished as we devote ourselves to exploring and understanding God's Word of truth, the Bible. And the converse is also true: Every time you say no to pursuing the knowledge of God and obeying His Word, your spiritual growth and the blessings that accompany it come to a halt.

Spiritual growth requires adversity. Many people wrongly assume that Christians should have problem-free lives. They become angry and disappointed when God does not keep them free of pain. They forget that Jesus Himself suffered pain and heartache His entire adult life, which ended in a cruel death. Jesus clearly warned us that "in this world you will have trouble." Yet He also went on to say, "But take heart! I have overcome the world" (John 16:33).

Adversity is for a Christian like exercise is for physical muscles. Without adversity, your spiritual muscles become weak as you come to depend more on yourself than upon God and His strength. Instead of trying to avoid trials or being angry with God when they arrive, determine to place your hardships into God's hands. Accept your difficult circumstances as opportunities for growth. And remember Paul's encouragement that "our light and momentary troubles are achieving for us an eternal glory that far outweighs them all" (2 Corinthians 4:17).

What Does This Mean for You?

Have you been viewing God's grace in salvation as an opportunity to sit back, take it easy, and "let God" work His magic in your life? Spiritual growth doesn't work that way. God saved you and began the work of sanctification through the Holy Spirit, who dwells in you. But you are still required to do your part. You are to "work out your salvation," to work at walking by the Spirit and living a godly and Christ-honoring life. All of this is going to cost you some pain to get the gain of spiritual growth.

No, you aren't working for your salvation. That's already been taken care of in Christ's death on your behalf. But you are to be laboring to honor and please God while He has you on this Earth. So "press on toward the goal to win the prize for which God has called [you] heavenward in Christ Jesus" (Philippians 3:13-14).

What is that prize? It is the most exciting aspect of sanctification—*ultimate sanctification*. This is what you will attain when you are fully and completely set apart to God in heaven. Therefore, you should gladly agree that in the spiritual life, no pain means no gain.

25

Give Yourself Grace...Because God Does

The law was given through Moses; grace
and truth came through Jesus Christ
(John 1:17).

All are justified freely by his grace through the
redemption that came by Christ Jesus
(Romans 3:24).

We believe it is through the grace of our
Lord Jesus that we are saved
(Acts 15:11).

*G*race. Just say the word, and many people begin to think of the words to the song "Amazing Grace." And truly, the story of John Newton, the writer of this hymn, is all about the amazing grace of God.

John Newton was a slave trader who plied his business in the 1700s. He was a rough and immoral man who later described himself as a "wretch"—which, from all accounts, he was...and more! Through a set of severe and life-threatening circumstances, Newton experienced a dramatic conversion that changed his heart and his way of life. He went on to become both a famous preacher and songwriter. No wonder he marveled in the first line of his hymn, "Amazing grace, how sweet the sound that saved a wretch like me!"

Grace is a central part of God's character and His dealings with mankind. Let's see what we can learn about His grace:

God's grace is undeserved. Have you ever done something bad—really bad? You knew you were wrong, and so did everyone else. And yet, your spouse, or your boss, or your family members were willing to forgive you. If this has happened to you, then to a small extent you have tasted what it means to receive mercy that was unjustified. That's what God's grace is! Simply put, grace is God's mercy, God's favor—God's unmerited favor.

From the very beginning of mankind, starting with Adam and Eve, God has demonstrated His favor. This couple willfully disobeyed God and deserved the punishment of death for their disobedience. But God showed them His grace—His favor—which was definitely unmerited!

Yes, Adam and Eve faced serious consequences for their sin. But God's grace was very much in evidence from the time they rebelled against Him. He provided coverings for their shame, and He sent them out of the garden to spare them contact with the tree of life which, if they had eaten from it while in their sinful state, would have resulted in eternal death and alienation without the possibility of redemption (Genesis 3:22-23). God has continued to dispense His grace to mankind since, and that grace is very much in evidence today. Every person who is a believer is living proof of God's mercy and grace!

God's grace saves. The Bible says that "all have sinned and fall short of the glory of God" (Romans 3:23), and that "the wages of sin is death" (Romans 6:23). Because all have sinned, no one deserves God's favor. But (here comes God's undeserved favor) "it is by grace you have been saved, through faith—and this is not from yourselves, it is the gift of God" (Ephesians 2:8).

Grace is God's intentional bestowal of His loving favor on those whom He saves. You and I cannot earn grace. If we could, it would no longer be unmerited or a "gift of God." And you cannot save yourself. Only God can save you. The only way for you to receive this gift of God's grace is by faith in Jesus Christ (Romans 3:24).

God's grace guides. Like John Newton, the apostle Paul was a despicable character before he met Jesus on the Damascus Road (Acts 9:1-9). He had persecuted and killed Christians. Yet even with his stained past, Paul could say, "By the grace of God I am what I am, and his grace to me was not without effect. No, I worked harder than all of them—yet not I, but the grace of God that was with me" (1 Corinthians 15:10).

God's grace reached down and changed Paul's life so thoroughly that he went from being a Christian-hater to being a Christian who loved his Lord and loved his brothers and sisters in Christ and was willing to suffer persecution for them. Paul recognized that it was only by God's guidance that he was able to accomplish anything good in his life. This transforming grace shaped and molded and guided him for many years as he represented Christ to people all across the Roman world.

That same grace and the guidance is given to each believer at salvation. God's grace gives us not only a new birth, but a new purpose and direction: "He has saved us and called us to a holy life—not because of anything we have done but because of his own purpose and grace. This grace was given us in Christ Jesus before the beginning of time" (2 Timothy 1:9).

God's grace empowers. The world is an unforgiving place, especially when it comes to living a godly life. You can be assured of facing at least some persecution (2 Timothy 3:12). As a Christian, you no longer share the world's values, and you are constantly in the position of guarding yourself against temptation and sin. On top of all that, we live in imperfect bodies that are prone to illness and suffering. So how do you cope with the various difficulties and obstacles so common in life? How do you gain the victory? The answer, again, is God's grace. Remember when the apostle Paul had to deal with what he called a "thorn in the flesh" (2 Corinthians 12:7)? He prayed to God, asking that it be removed. What was God's response to Paul? "My grace is sufficient for you for my power is made perfect in weakness" (verse 9).

What Does This Mean for You?

It is an understatement to say that the Christian life is not easy. In fact, you could say that it is impossible. Like so many believers before you, including people like the apostle Paul, you will experience weaknesses, insults, distresses, persecution, and difficulties. But take heart! God promises that the grace that saved you will also be the grace that keeps you and provides the strength and power you need to live the Christian life. God's grace comes through His indwelling Spirit, who will guide and empower you. No matter what your situation, you can approach God's throne of grace with confidence, so that you may receive mercy and find grace to help you in your time of need (Hebrews 4:16).

Now, what part can you play in putting God's G-R-A-C-E to work in your life?

> **G**-ive thanks to God that you are under grace and not the law.
>
> **R**-espond in love and obedience to the gift of God's grace in your life.
>
> **A**-sk God for wisdom to understand what His grace should mean in your life.
>
> **C**-ommune with other believers in a Bible-teaching church where you can receive training in the ways of God.
>
> **E**-xtend God's grace to others by sharing the gospel, showing forgiveness, and helping them to shoulder their burdens.

26

This World Is Not Your Home

*Our citizenship is in heaven. And we eagerly await
a Savior from there, the Lord Jesus Christ
(Philippians 3:20).*

*My Father's house has many rooms; if that were
not so, would I have told you that I am going there
to prepare a place for you? And if I go and prepare
a place for you, I will come back and take you to
be with me that you also may be where I am
(John 14:2-3).*

*Do not rejoice that the spirits submit to you, but
rejoice that your names are written in heaven
(Luke 10:20).*

A number of years ago, the church I attended commissioned me and my family for a missions ministry in the country of Singapore. We went through all the usual procedures for getting visas to live and minister in that country. We left the United States not knowing when we might return, and we were prepared to stay as long as we were needed by the people who had invited us.

Rather than live in the area where most Westerners resided, we moved into an all-Chinese community. My wife walked to the local market each day for food, and after my daughters were finished with school, I would often find them sitting at one of the local outdoor food stalls, enjoying a Coke and eating a Chinese pastry. We were residents and lived with the local people, yet at the same time we were citizens of another country. Even though we loved the people and enjoyed the culture, we knew Singapore wasn't our true home. We were sojourners, aliens in a foreign land.

Our family's situation in Singapore illustrates perfectly the situation Christians are in while living on Earth. This world is not our home. We are only visitors, and our true citizenship is in heaven. What does this citizenship in God's kingdom look like?

Citizenship in heaven is exclusive. Jesus made a promise to His disciples: "I go and prepare a place for you, I will come back and take you to be with me that you also may be where I am" (John 14:3). Only those who are believers in Jesus will be taken to God's heavenly kingdom. In fact, Revelation 21:27 lists for us the kind of people who will populate this kingdom: "Nothing impure will ever enter [the New Jerusalem], nor will anyone who does what is shameful or deceitful, but only those whose names are written in the Lamb's book of life."

Citizenship in heaven is eternal. Your citizenship in an earthly kingdom began the day of your birth, and that citizenship will end the day you die. Similarly, your citizenship in God's kingdom begins at your "new birth" in Christ, but unlike your citizenship here on Earth, it will never end. Rather, it will last for all eternity. As Jesus said, "I give them eternal life, and they shall never perish; no one will snatch them out of my hand" (John 10:28). Human governments and earthly kingdoms come and go, but God's kingdom is eternal. And you, as a spiritual citizen of that kingdom, will live forever with your King.

Citizenship in heaven brings immediate benefits. In Colossians 1:12-14, we read of five immediate benefits for those who become citizens of God's kingdom:

1. We are qualified to share in Christ's inheritance in the kingdom (verse 12).

2. We are rescued from the dominion of darkness (verse 13).

3. We are brought into the kingdom of the Son of God (verse 13).

4. We are redeemed from sin and judgment (verse 14).

5. We are forgiven of all our sins (verse 14).

Citizenship in heaven means representing Christ on Earth. When you live in a foreign country, you represent your native country to the people around you—you are a reflection of your home country. It is the same way with your citizenship in God's kingdom. You are to reflect the Father and His Son, the Lord Jesus, to those around you here on Earth. The apostle Paul wrote, "We are therefore Christ's ambassadors, as though God were making his appeal through us" (2 Corinthians 5:20). Wherever we live or roam, we represent Christ and are instruments of His work. And we must live in a way that ensures others are seeing a true representation of Christ.

Citizenship in heaven comes with a tutor. When a person immigrates to a new country and wants to become a citizen, he must take a class and learn the basic governing laws and regulations of their new country. Sometimes immigrants find it beneficial to get the help of a tutor who can prepare them for taking the exam that must be passed in order to become a citizen.

God knows that you, as a citizen of His kingdom, need someone to help you be a proper representative and a fruitful citizen while you are still on Earth. Therefore, He has provided the Holy Spirit as your guide, your helper, your teacher until you make the transition to heaven (John 14:26).

Citizenship in heaven demands godly living on Earth. As Christians, we are foreigners on Earth because our real home is in heaven. And we have the privilege of representing God to a watching world. It was this Peter had in mind when he wrote, "Dear friends, I urge you, as foreigners and exiles, to abstain from sinful desires...Live such good lives among the pagans that, though they accuse you of doing wrong, they may see your good deeds and glorify God on the day he visits us" (1 Peter 2:11-12).

Citizenship in heaven produces model citizens on Earth. None of the writers of the New Testament commented negatively on the Roman government and its many injustices. Jesus didn't engage in any criticism either. In fact, He told the people to give the government its due in taxes. Paul wrote that believers are to obey the governing authorities (Romans 13:1), and Peter said we are to submit to every human authority (1 Peter 2:13).

Citizenship in heaven will promote peace on Earth. "The beatitudes" spoken by Jesus give a description of righteous living for kingdom citizens (see Matthew 5:3-12). All the beatitudes are important, but in a world filled with war and violence, there is no better way to be God's representatives than through promoting peace. Jesus said, "Blessed are the peacemakers, for they will be called children of God" (Matthew 5:9). Paul conveyed the same message in a more practical way: "If it is possible, as far as it depends on you, live at peace with everyone" (Romans 12:18).

What Does This Mean for You?

As a Christian, you are a citizen of heaven, even though you currently reside here on Earth. Your citizenship—which will last for all eternity—cost the death of God's Son and should not be taken lightly or for granted. Life on Earth may seem wonderful, but as the apostle Paul said, you should eagerly look forward to your home in heaven. At the same time, as with so many other things in the Christian life, the matter of your citizenship requires balance. Yes, you are to live in eager anticipation of heaven. But while you wait, you are to stay busy working for Christ, loving the lost, and leading the life of a model earthly citizen. With this balance, you will have the best of both worlds!

27

God Is Real and He Is Not Silent

God said, "Let there be light," and there was light
(Genesis 1:3).

By the word of the LORD the heavens were made,
their starry host by the breath of his mouth
(Psalm 33:6).

In the past God spoke to our ancestors through the prophets
at many times and in various ways, but in these last days
he has spoken to us by his Son, whom he appointed heir of
all things, and through whom also he made the universe
(Hebrews 1:1-2).

How do we know there is a God? "There must be," you say, "because so many people groups and individuals from the beginning of recorded history have believed in some 'higher power,' something—or someone—they call god." Anyone who gives any honest thought to the immensity of the universe, the complexity of life, and the grandeur and beauty of the Earth cannot help but look beyond themselves for answers.

If there is a God, and most people would say there is, then we would expect that at some point God would let His existence be known. Why would this great being called God simply create the universe and walk away, having no other interaction with His creation? That would be the same as parents walking away from their child, leaving the child to fend for itself.

God has not done that! Rather than leaving mankind with no further information about Himself, He took the initiative and revealed Himself in two significant ways.

First, God revealed Himself through what is called *general revelation*. Through general revelation, God has spoken to man indirectly—that is, through creation, history, and the human personality.

God has marked His presence for anyone who wishes to observe it. Regardless of whether a person makes the effort to observe His presence, understand it, or believe it, God's handiwork is on display for all to see. General revelation is often the starting point in a person's journey toward discovering God. However, general revelation does not give mankind a personal knowledge of God.

God has also revealed Himself through what is known as *special revelation*. Through the ages, He has shown Himself to certain people at specific times and places, enabling those persons to enter into a special relationship with Him. These encounters are recorded in the Bible, through which God speaks to people directly.

One theologian explains special revelation this way:

> There exists one Triune God, loving, all-powerful, holy, all-knowing, who has revealed himself in nature, history, and human personality, and in those acts and words which are now preserved in the canonical Scriptures of the Old and New Testaments.[1]

One expression that appears in the Bible multiple times is the statement, "The word of the LORD came to me, saying..." This "word" could take on several forms. Some revelations were audibly spoken. Other were silent, inward hearings of God's message, or were communicated by dreams. But in all cases, the recipient knew the revelation was coming from God. Yes, God is real, and He is not silent. He has spoken. Here are a few of the ways God has spoken to His people.

The creation. Most scientists have yet to do more than develop "theories" to explain the existence of the universe and the rational, intellectual creature called man. By contrast, the very first verse of the Bible states, "In the beginning God created the heavens and the earth" (Genesis 1:1). Verse 3 continues, "And God said, 'Let there be light,' and there was light." God literally spoke the universe into existence (Psalm 33:6). So when a person looks to the heavens, he is viewing God's handiwork on display. The universe didn't just pop into existence on its own. God made it happen!

A key part of God's creative work was making man in His own image (verse 26). This marked the beginning of God's special and direct involvement with mankind. And God didn't stop there.

The flood. Later, God revealed Himself to a righteous man named Noah. God "spoke" again, telling Noah to build an ark to save himself, his family, and some animals. God told Noah the reason for the ark: "I am going to put an end to all people, for the earth is filled with violence because of them. I am surely going to destroy both them and the earth" (Genesis 6:13). Through direct communication, God made known the fact He would preserve a remnant of people from a worldwide flood.

The creation of the nation of Israel. Through direct communication, God directed a man named Abram to move to a new land, where he would become the father of a new nation—Israel. God continued this personal communication with Abraham's descendants up through the time of Moses, who helped lead God's people out of Egypt. Then, in dramatic fashion, God again spoke to Moses and etched the Ten Commandments on tablets of stones. These were God's standards for His people to live by. Ultimately, the people of Israel settled in a land promised to them by God, and from this people would come the greatest of all revelations— Jesus Christ.

The birth of Jesus. Theologians call Jesus' birth the *incarnation,* meaning "to enter into or become flesh." The doctrine of the incarnation states that the pre-existent Son of God became a man, Jesus. The book of Hebrews gives a great summary of God's revelation through historical events and divine speech, as well as His work through Jesus: "God, who at various times and in various ways spoke in time past to the fathers by the prophets, has in these last days spoken to us by His Son" (Hebrews 1:1-2 NKJV).

Jesus, as God in human flesh. was the ultimate spokesman for God. God is spirit, so His Son took on human flesh to personally speak to man. Jesus was the walking revelation of God as He spoke God's words and performed God's wondrous acts, including the crucifixion and resurrection. This last act made it possible for the coming of God's Spirit, who would speak to the hearts of all those who would receive Jesus as their personal Savior.

What Does This Mean for You?

Secrets are sometimes necessary to help protect people or things. But when it comes to God's existence and His desire to communicate to and have a relationship with people, there is no secret—God does exist! He has communicated to us indirectly through His creation, and He has communicated to us directly through His Word, the Bible, and especially through His Son, the Lord Jesus.

Yes, God is here and He is not silent. If you are not yet a Christian, the question for you to ask is this: "Do I recognize that there is a God and He is revealing Himself to me, and that He desires for me to welcome Him into my life?" God is offering you salvation and the gift of eternal life through His Son (John 10:28).

If you have responded to God's revelation of Himself through Jesus, praise and thank Him for your salvation. Get to know Him even better through His Word. Talk to Him through prayer. Worship Him in your heart and at church. And share His message of salvation with those who do not have a relationship with Him. Exult with the saints of the Old Testament, "The LORD is my strength and my defense; he has become my salvation. He is my God, and I will praise him" (Exodus 15:2).

Note

1 Bernard Ramm, *Protestant Christian Evidences* (Chicago: Moody, 1953), p. 33; as cited in Millard J. Erickson, *Christian Theology* (Grand Rapids: Baker, 1983), p. 33.

28

Sin Is Not Just an Action,
but a Nature

*All have sinned and fall short of the glory of God
(Romans 3:23).*

*I know that good itself does not dwell in me, that
is, in my sinful nature. For I have the desire to
do what is good, but I cannot carry it out
(Romans 7:18).*

*Thanks be to God, who delivers me through Jesus Christ
our Lord! So then, I myself in my mind am a slave to God's
law, but in my sinful nature a slave to the law of sin
(Romans 7:25).*

The world is a scary place, not just because of global political unrest that includes wars, terrorism, kidnappings, and assassinations. The world is also filled with natural disasters and scary diseases. Two examples of frightening diseases are the Ebola virus (also known as EHF, or Ebola Hemorrhagic Fever) and AIDS, both of which have brought about major devastation to Africa. What makes these diseases particularly terrifying is that they are deadly, and it's been so difficult to find a cure for them.

One disease for which there is no human cure is sin. But unlike a disease that you catch when you come into contact with a person or a virus, sin infects every person from birth, including you. It is embedded in our nature. There is no physical cure for it, and it eats away at us until we die.

Thankfully, *God* has provided us with a cure for sin. In Mark 2, we see Jesus apply this cure to a paralytic man who was brought to Jesus by his friends. At the time, Jesus was teaching inside a house, surrounded by a crowd that spilled out the door. Because the friends were unable to reach Jesus, they climbed onto the roof of the house, made an opening, and lowered the paralytic man so that he ended up at Jesus' feet. When Jesus saw their faith, he said to the paralyzed man, "Son, your sins are forgiven" (Mark 2:5).

Some of the religious leaders who heard Jesus say this exclaimed, "He's blaspheming! Who can forgive sins but God alone?" (verse 7).

Jesus answered, "The Son of Man has authority on earth to forgive sins" (verse 10). Only Christ's healing touch can deal with the incurable sin nature that infects body and soul.

As we saw earlier in this book, every person is a sinner. Sin isn't just our actions. Rather, it's a part of our nature—it's who we are. Let's see what Scripture has to say about this.

The sin nature had a beginning. In medical science, the "index case" or "initial patient" in the population of an epidemic outbreak is labeled "patient zero." In the book of Genesis, Adam became "patient zero" with respect to the introduction of sin into the world. Here's how the Bible describes the outbreak of this epidemic: God created the perfect universe complete with two perfect people, Adam and Eve. They could do anything except eat the fruit of one particular tree. God had warned them, "You must not eat from the tree of the knowledge of good and evil, for when you eat from it you will certainly die" (Genesis 2:17).

When Adam ate the forbidden fruit given to him by Eve, who had already eaten it herself, he became a sinner. Sin, by definition, is anything that is contrary to God's standard. It is missing God's mark; it is anything less than perfection. When Adam and Eve ate the forbidden fruit, they willfully disobeyed God.

Immediately, Adam was completely infected with sin. He was

no longer perfect. He was flawed in his nature, and he passed this flaw on to everyone who has been born since. The apostle Paul explained the outbreak this way: "Just as sin entered the world through one man, and death through sin…in this way death came to all people, because all sinned" (Romans 5:12). Because of what Adam had done, sin was now running loose in the world.

The sin nature operates without restraints. The natural man has no personal connection with God and "does not receive the things of the Spirit of God, for they are foolishness to him; nor can he know them, because they are spiritually discerned" (1 Corinthians 2:14 NKJV). Without any spiritual input from God, an unsaved person has no restraints other than his society's norms and a warped conscience. He operates solely through his fleshly desires. The Bible lists his normal or "evident" activities as "adultery, fornication, uncleanness, lewdness, idolatry, sorcery, hatred, contentions, jealousies, outbursts of wrath, selfish ambitions, dissensions, heresies" (Galatians 5:19-20).

Not a pretty picture, is it? Unless God intervenes in a person's life, his sin nature will condemn him to death and eternity apart from God (Romans 6:23).

The sin nature has a rival. Man's sin nature had its origin in Adam. As a result, man is spiritually dead in trespasses and sin. People sin because they are sinners. Sinful behavior is what people do naturally without God. As we have seen, the only rival for the sin nature is Jesus Christ.

Through Jesus' sacrificial death on the cross, there is now a remedy for sin. People have a choice. They can either choose to follow God, or reject Him. They can, through faith in Christ, put off their "old self" and its sinful behavior, as if they were removing an old coat. And they can put on the "new self," which acts "like God in true righteousness and holiness" (Ephesians 4:22-24).

The sin nature battles with godliness. In Romans 7, the apostle Paul wrote about the struggle every believer has with sin. Here, he speaks from personal experience. You can sense his frustration as he describes the conflict within himself—the conflict between his old sin nature and his desire as a new man to honor God. He condemns his corrupt nature with its affections and lusts and its desires to do evil: "I have the desire to do what is good, but I cannot carry it out. For I do not do the good I want to do, but the evil I do not want to do—this I keep on doing" (Romans 7:17-19).

The sin nature can be overcome. In Romans 7:17-24, Paul explains that the struggle between the old life and new continues even after one becomes a Christian. The old nature doesn't disappear with salvation. It is still present in our flesh. But as Christians, we are capable of rejecting its influence. Paul said we have two options: One, we can allow ourselves to be influenced by "the desires of the flesh" (Galatians 5:16). Or two, we can "walk by the Spirit" (verse 16).

As believers, we can have victory over the desires of the flesh by walking according to the Holy Spirit—by obeying God's Word and thereby producing the fruit of the Spirit (verses 22-23). This does not mean we won't sin. It just means we can now choose to either walk by the Spirit or give in to the flesh.

Tragically, the only choice unbelievers have is to do "the acts of the flesh," and if they remain unsaved, they "will not inherit the kingdom of God" (verse 21).

What Does This Mean for You?

For an unbeliever, there is no battle against the sin nature. An unbeliever sins because that is his nature. But as a believer, you have a choice whether to sin or not. Unfortunately, Satan disguises sin as delightful, fun, and exciting. The Bible says, "Be alert and of sober mind. Your enemy the devil prowls around like a roaring lion looking for someone to devour" (1 Peter 5:8). So prepare yourself for the many attractive temptations that will come your way. See them for what they are—enticing invitations to fall into ugly sins.

Do you want to avoid sinning? Then do these two things:

> "Submit yourselves, then, to God. Resist the devil,
> and he will flee from you" (James 4:7).

29

It's Really All About Love

*God so loved the world that he gave his one
and only Son, that whoever believes in him
shall not perish but have eternal life
(John 3:16).*

*Hope does not put us to shame, because God's
love has been poured out into our hearts through
the Holy Spirit, who has been given to us
(Romans 5:5).*

L ove has to be one of the most misunderstood emotions, attitudes, and qualities we as humans desire and possess. The world by and large wants to define love as some sort of physical attraction with the exclusion of just about everything else. But the Bible has another way of looking at love and measuring it. And we should listen to what it has to say, because it speaks extensively of love, using the word more than 680 times. Furthermore, in the Bible we see a perfect person who demonstrates to us God's definition of love—Jesus Christ. But before we learn about love from Jesus, let's see how the Bible describes love from the perspective of God the Father.

God shows us love. Love is both a divine quality within the nature of the Trinity as well as an activity each member of the Trinity performs. For instance, here are some facts about God's love:

God's love is part of His nature: "God is love" (1 John 4:8).

God's love for His Son is from all eternity—"you loved me before the creation of the world" (John 17:24).

God's love is active—"he gave his one and only Son" (John 3:16).

God's love is enduring—"neither height nor depth, nor anything else in all creation, will be able to separate us from the love of God that is in Christ Jesus our Lord" (Romans 8:39).

God's love includes those who are lost—"for the Son of Man has come to seek and to save the lost" (Luke 19:10).

God's love is sacrificial—"God demonstrates his own love for us in this: While we were still sinners, Christ died for us" (Romans 5:8).

God's love blesses His children—"see what great love the Father has lavished on us, that we should be called children of God!" (1 John 3:1).

God's love is everlasting—"I have loved you with an everlasting love" (Jeremiah 31:3).

Jesus teaches about love. In Jesus we find both the greatest model of love and our ultimate resource for loving others. He loved perfectly, and He teaches—and commands—us to do the same. Hear now the Master Teacher's instruction on love!

Jesus practiced love—Because He perfectly practiced love, Jesus shows us how to do the same and live out His command to "love one another" (John 13:34).

Jesus loved His friends—We read in John 11:5 that "Jesus loved Martha and her sister and Lazarus." We see Him in their home having meals on several occasions and arriving to offer His help after Lazarus's death. As a friend, Jesus was there when these friends needed Him in a life or death crisis.

Jesus loved His fellow workers—John, who is referred to as the disciple "whom Jesus loved" (John 13:23), gives this insight into the love Jesus had for the Twelve: "Jesus knew that the hour had come for him to leave this world and go to the Father. Having loved his own who were in the world, he loved them to the end" (John 13:1). To the end! Loving your family and friends is one thing, but how about those you work with every day?

Jesus loved the lost—Luke 19:10 says, "The Son of Man came to seek and to save the lost." Jesus actively mingled with the lost. He didn't avoid them. He sought out those who had needs.

Jesus' love was sacrificial—Jesus took love to its ultimate test when He willingly died on the cross to secure our salvation. He gave the greatest example ever of unselfish and sacrificial love. Jesus was speaking of Himself when He said, "Greater love has no one than this: to lay down one's life for one's friends" (John 15:13).

How can you show the kind of love Jesus showed? It all begins with a personal relationship with God through Jesus Christ. Once you are a child of God, as you spend time in His Word and in prayer, you will receive His love anew each day. From there the love moves out in caring attitudes and actions toward family first, then to other believers, and finally to the world, to any and all who cross our path. Because of the indwelling Holy Spirit, Christians have God's love to give—to love God first, and then love others.

What Does This Mean for You?

Love is costly. God's love cost the death of His Son. God's love asks that you surrender your sin and accept His Son as your Savior. Christ's love asks you to practice sacrificial love in some very practical ways...like listening, helping, serving, encouraging, and giving of your time and money.

Have you ever thought about why Jesus commands you to love? Love requires something of you. It takes effort. And sadly, love is not always a normal response, unless perhaps you're a parent. But beyond this familial bond, love must be nurtured. It must be nudged a bit, especially if you are hesitating to reach out in love, maybe because you were hurt at some time in the past when you tried loving another person.

In spite of any obstacle that keeps you from being obedient to God's command to love, you can—and need—to recall how deeply you are loved by God through His Son, Jesus, in spite of your sins and faults. His unconditional love should move you to love others. It shows you the way to love. Realizing how much God loves you will help you to overcome your reluctance to love others. Then, as you demonstrate love toward others, the feeling of love will follow naturally.

30

Jesus Really Is Coming Back

*"Men of Galilee," they said, "why do you stand here
looking into the sky? This same Jesus, who has been
taken from you into heaven, will come back in the
same way you have seen him go into heaven"
(Acts 1:10–11).*

*Dear friends, now we are children of God, and what
we will be has not yet been made known. But we
know that when Christ appears, we shall be like
him, for we shall see him as he is. All who have this
hope in him purify themselves, just as he is pure
(1 John 3:2–3).*

*I saw heaven standing open and there before me was
a white horse, whose rider is called Faithful and True.
With justice he judges and wages war. His eyes are
like blazing fire, and on his head are many crowns
(Revelation 19:11–12).*

The Bible is a precise book. It contains only what God decided
is important for us to know. Therefore, when something is
repeated, we can be assured God wants to get our attention. One
example of this is the number of times the Old Testament pre-
dicted Christ's personal, visible return to reign upon the Earth.

There are more prophecies about His return than any other subject. And in the New Testament, which has 260 chapters, Jesus' second coming is mentioned 318 times. More specifically, Jesus' return is mentioned once in every 25 verses. Obviously God is alerting us to the importance of the fact of Jesus' return. How, then, should we respond?

Unfortunately, the wonderful promise of Jesus' return is obscured by the confusion many people have about the events surrounding Christ's second coming. There are two schools of thought about His return:

One group believes the return of Christ will happen in two stages: First, Jesus will come from heaven and take up Christians to return with Him to heaven. This event is referred to as "the rapture of the church" and is described in 1 Thessalonians 4:13-18. The second stage comes at the end of seven years of what is called "the Great Tribulation," when Jesus will come back in great glory. This stage is described in Revelation 19. At this return Jesus will eradicate all His enemies and Christians will reign with Him for 1000 years in what is called the millennial kingdom.

Other Bible teachers are convinced that the rapture and the glorious return are the same event. They don't see two stages in Christ's return.

Regardless of which way you lean, it is impossible to miss the great emphasis the New Testament places on the fact Jesus is coming back. That, of course, leads to the next question: What will happen at Christ's return?

Jesus' second coming has a different purpose. The purpose of Jesus' first mission was to come as a servant and Savior. He came to show people the way to salvation and eternal life. But the second time He comes, He will come in judgment to condemn all those who rejected His offer of salvation.

Jesus' second coming will complete the reality of salvation. Believers are assured that there is "no condemnation for those who are in Christ Jesus" (Romans 8:1). First Corinthians 1:8 says that God "will also keep you firm to the end, so that you will be blameless on the day of our Lord Jesus Christ." This guarantee is not because of our great gifts or our stellar actions, but because of what Jesus Christ accomplished for us through His death and resurrection.

Jesus' second coming is for the purpose of gathering up His own. Those who comprise the church will be gathered together by Jesus to return with Him to heaven. They will instantly be transformed into their eternal bodies. Jesus gave His disciples—and all believers—this assurance: "If I go and prepare a place for you, I will come back and take you to be with me that you also may be where I am" (John 14:3).

Jesus' second coming will include the resurrection of believers who have died. The question posed by the Thessalonian church was, What will happen to those who have already died before Christ returns? Paul wrote to help them understand that death, for the believer, was not the end. When Christ returns, all believers, including those who had already died, will be reunited, never to suffer or die again (1 Thessalonians 4:13-14).

With this information about what will happen at Jesus' second coming, you can now ask this more practical question: "How should I live while I await Jesus' return?"

What Does This Mean for You?

Jesus said that no person knows the time of His return: "About that day or hour no one knows, not even the angels in heaven" (Matthew 24:36). This means we should always be prepared for His second coming. But that doesn't mean we can ignore what is going on around us right now. At the same time that we keep one eye on the sky, we should also give full attention to our responsibilities as Christians here on Earth. We are to fulfill our obligations, care for our families and loved ones, and live in a way that draws other people to God. We should also be diligent about sharing the message of salvation with the lost. That was the disciples' mission, and it is yours too (Matthew 28:19-20). Because you don't know the date of Christ's return, there should be a sense of urgency on your part to spread the good news while there is still time.

Finally, the prophecies about Jesus' return were not written to satisfy your curiosity about the future, but to change the way you live here on Earth. This was the apostle Peter's concern for his readers, and it should be your concern as well: "Beloved, since you look for these things, be diligent to be found by Him in peace, spotless and blameless" (2 Peter 3:14 NASB).

31

Jesus Prays for You and Me

*After the Lord Jesus had spoken to them, he was taken
up into heaven and he sat at the right hand of God
(Mark 16:19).*

*There is one God and one mediator between
God and mankind, the man Christ Jesus
(1 Timothy 2:5).*

*He raised Christ from the dead and seated him
at his right hand in the heavenly realms
(Ephesians 1:20).*

Historically, Bible scholars have categorized the work of
Christ in terms of three "offices" or "functions." These are
prophet, priest, and king. While these offices or functions may
be spoken of in distinct terms, they cannot be divorced from one
another. Jesus, the Son of God, may have entered this world as one
who preached and prophesied things to come, but He was still a
king who was yet to receive His kingdom. And He functioned as
a priest, often praying for His disciples, and offering the ultimate
sacrifice of Himself on the cross. In this chapter we will focus on
the teaching about Jesus' function as intercessory priest—the fact
that *Jesus prays for you.*

Jesus' intercession has its roots in the Old Testament. God instituted the office of priest shortly after the children of Israel left Egypt (Exodus 28). The priests (and particularly the high priest) were to intercede for the people and offer sacrifices for their sins. Also, once a year, the high priest offered a sacrifice for the sins of the entire nation on the Day of Atonement. Originally these sacrifices and other priestly functions were conducted in and around the mobile structure called the tabernacle, and later they were done at a stationary temple in Jerusalem. But with the coming of Jesus Christ, the Messiah, the office of high priest became obsolete. Why? Because Jesus assumed this role.

Jesus' intercession was permanent. With the destruction of the temple in Jerusalem by the Romans in AD 70, the Jewish religion no longer had a facility for the functions of its Old Testament priesthood. Without a temple, Jewish priests could no longer continue to intercede for the people. The early church was made up of Jews who had converted to Christianity, and because of their Jewish background, these converts were familiar with the role of the priest and could easily grasp the fact that Jesus was now their priest and intercessor. The book of Hebrews, which was written to Jewish people across the Roman world, makes this very clear when it says, "Now there have been many of those priests, since death prevented them from continuing in office; but because Jesus lives forever, he has a permanent priesthood" (Hebrews 7:23-24).

Jesus' intercession began during His earthly ministry. Again, one of the roles of the Old Testament priests was to intercede for the people. Twice a day they would enter the holy place of the temple and burn incense as a prayer offering for the people's sin. Similarly, while on Earth, Jesus would often pray for His disciples.

On the night before His death, Jesus lifted up a lengthy intercessory prayer on behalf of His disciples. This prayer, which appears in John 17, marks the transition from Jesus' earthly ministry to the beginning of His intercessory ministry for all believers in heaven, as described in Hebrews 7:25: "He is able to save completely those who come to God through him, because he always lives to intercede for them."

Jesus' intercession comes with authority. Ever since Jesus' ascension in Acts chapter 1, He has been seated at the right hand of the Father. The significance of Jesus' position is that the right hand is the place of distinction and power—it is not a place of rest or inactivity. That He is at the right hand of the Father is a symbol of authority and active rule. It is at this place that Jesus intercedes to the Father on your behalf: "There is one God and one mediator between God and mankind, the man Christ Jesus" (1 Timothy 2:5).

Jesus' intercession is ongoing. Jesus did not simply give us eternal life and then abandon us to our human self-efforts. Rather, the work that Jesus began with His priestly intercession for His disciples and the sacrifice of Himself on the cross will continue until it is completed—when His followers enter into His presence. "Being confident of this, that he who began a good work in you will carry it on to completion until the day of Christ Jesus" (Philippians 1:6).

As we saw in Hebrews 7:25, Christ is making intercession for all believers continually. John 11:42 indicates that the Father always hears Jesus' prayers, so we can be certain that Jesus' prayers for all believers will continue to sustain them until they get to heaven.

Jesus' intercession is focused. We have a limited understanding of Jesus' role as our advocate and intercessor. But in John 17:11-26, we are given a glimpse of Jesus' love and care for His own as He prayed first for His disciples, and then for all those who would become believers from that time onward. Surely that is the same love and care He expresses today as He intercedes on our behalf.

Note the specifics of Jesus' prayer:

First, Jesus prayed for His disciples (John 17:11-17):

1. He asks that the Father unify them.

2. He asks that the Father impart joy to them.

3. He asks that the Father protect them.

4. He asks that the Father sanctify them.

Then Jesus prayed for all who would believe in Him (John 17:20-24):

1. He asks that believers show unity.

2. He asks that believers honor the Son.

3. He asks that believers display God's love.

4. He asks that believers experience God's love.

5. He asks that believers enjoy Christ's glory in heaven forever.

The fact that Jesus prays and intercedes for us should be a source of comfort. We are His beloved followers, and He is praying to the Father that we be a united force in the world. He is praying that we will "love one another" (1 John 4:7). His desire is that we would live in unity and love with one purpose in mind: "Then the world will know that [the Father] sent me" (verse 23). Our loving and unified testimony will proclaim to others that Jesus was sent by the Father as Savior of the world.

What Does This Mean for You?

The pattern of Jesus' intercessory prayer for His disciples and all believers can provide a helpful outline for your own prayers. Also, the fact Jesus is constantly interceding on your behalf does not mean you should stop praying for yourself and your concerns. It just means that when you come boldly before the Father's throne with your requests, you have an intercessor and mediator who accompanies you.

Let Jesus' intercessory prayer help bring more focus to your own prayers:

Pray for yourself, your needs, and your spiritual growth.

Pray for others to be saved and to love the Lord.

Pray for unity among Christians and your part in promoting unity.

32

When Jesus Died, So Did Death

*What I received I passed on to you as of first
importance: that Christ died for our sins according
to the Scriptures, that he was buried, that he was
raised on the third day according to the Scriptures
(1 Corinthians 15:3–4).*

*Don't you know that all of us who were baptized into
Christ Jesus were baptized into his death? We were
therefore buried with him through baptism into death in
order that, just as Christ was raised from the dead through
the glory of the Father, we too may live a new life. For if
we have been united with him in a death like his, we will
certainly also be united with him in a resurrection like his
(Romans 6:3–5).*

These are our core values as a company." I can't tell you how many times I heard or read this statement when I was in the business world. What exactly are core values? They summarize, in a few words, a company's goals and purposes. They help keep a company focused in a certain direction with specific objectives in mind. And a key benefit of core values is that they can inspire employees toward exceptional performance.

When it comes to Christianity, there's a sense in which we could say Christ's resurrection is the "core value." The resurrection is the focal point of every truth Christ taught His disciples while on Earth. He said, "I am the resurrection and the life. The one who believes in me will live, even though they die" (John 11:25). The first two sermons preached after Christ's resurrection and ascension focused on His resurrection (see Acts 2:14-36 and 3:12-26). It was the resurrection that turned Jesus' brokenhearted followers into courageous witnesses and martyrs who, in just a few years, spread the gospel across the Roman Empire and beyond. And ultimately, the resurrection proclaimed the fact that when Jesus died, so did death.

Jesus died to buy you back from the bondage of sin. Jesus frequently told His disciples that He must die, and He told them why: "The Son of Man did not come to be served, but to serve, and to give his life as a ransom for many" (Matthew 20:28). A ransom was the price paid to release a slave from bondage.

When Adam and Eve sinned in the Garden of Eden, mankind came under the bondage of Satan, sin, and death. Jesus' death paid the ransom price that was necessary to satisfy God's holiness and justice. God's holiness required that the penalty be paid, and God's love provided that payment in the death of the Son (John 3:16). Jesus' perfect life was the only sacrifice that could be offered that would satisfy God's justice. Jesus died so you don't have to die.

Jesus died to prove His power over death. Jesus had to die not only to pay the penalty for our sin, but also to show His power over death. The apostle Paul said Jesus "was appointed the Son of God in power by his resurrection from the dead" (Romans 1:3-4). Jesus' resurrection from the dead proves He is God and that He possesses eternal life, and that He can therefore give this same eternal life to all who believe in Him.

Jesus died defeating death. At first glance, Satan appeared to be victorious in the Garden of Eden (Genesis 3). Adam and Eve had disobeyed God, and their sin resulted in immediate spiritual death and ultimate physical death. Even at the cross, when Jesus died, Satan seemed to have won. But God turned Satan's apparent victory into defeat when Jesus rose from the dead. Death is no longer a source of dread or fear for us—it "has been swallowed up in victory" (1 Corinthians 15:54).

> "Where, O death, is your victory? Where, O death, is your sting?" The sting of death is sin, and the power of sin is the law. But thanks be to God! He gives us the victory through our Lord Jesus Christ (1 Corinthians 15:55-57).

Christ overcame death, and there is coming a day when all those who are in Christ will overcome it too.

Jesus died to give hope. Many of the world's religions speak of some sort of life after death. But what they say about the afterlife is filled with uncertainty. They offer a hope that is unsure, a hope that has no substance. Only Christianity gives a certain hope that death has been conquered, a hope based on actual eyewitness accounts of the bodily resurrection of Jesus. Paul was one of these eyewitnesses and he gives a list of people who saw Jesus alive after He was confirmed dead by the Roman guards—men who were experts in dealing out death. Here's Paul's list:

> He appeared to Cephas, and then to the Twelve. After that, he appeared to more than five hundred of the brothers and sisters at the same time, most of whom are still living, though some have fallen asleep. Then he appeared to James, then to all the apostles, and last of all he appeared to me also, as to one abnormally born (1 Corinthians 15:5-8).

Death was defeated at the cross. Jesus is alive! Death no longer holds any power over Him or His followers. No other religion can make this statement:

> Christ has indeed been raised from the dead, the firstfruits of those who have fallen asleep. For since

death came through a man, the resurrection of the dead comes also through a man. For as in Adam all die, so in Christ all will be made alive (1 Corinthians 15:20-22).

Jesus' death cancelled spiritual death. All people die physically, but Christ died so believers would not experience spiritual death. Christians can have the utmost confidence in Christ's saving work and their eternal life. At the moment of salvation, we are declared righteous before God. And as Romans 8:1 says, "There is now no condemnation for those who are in Christ Jesus." As believers in Christ, we have no reason to fear death.

What Does This Mean for You?

Are you a believer in Christ? If so, you will not experience spiritual death. How should this affect you? For starters, you should be thankful! Also, realize that even though you possess eternal life, you are still functioning in a perishable body. You don't know how much time you have left on Earth. So make the most of the time you have by serving God and His people. Your new life is not meant to be spent in self-indulgence. With that in mind, take to heart the apostle Paul's challenge to "stand firm. Let nothing move you. Always give yourselves fully to the work of the Lord, because you know that your labor in the Lord is not in vain" (1 Corinthians 15:58).

33

One Birth Is Not Enough

He saved us through the washing of rebirth
and renewal by the Holy Spirit
(Titus 3:5).

Praise be to the God and Father of our Lord Jesus Christ!
In his great mercy he has given us new birth into a living
hope through the resurrection of Jesus Christ from the dead
(1 Peter 1:3).

If you know that he is righteous, you know that everyone
who does what is right has been born of him
(1 John 2:29).

With the stagnation of many mainline church denominations during the 1960s, a wave of countercultural young people branded as "Jesus freaks" were becoming Christians. This new generation of believers realized the deadness of their churches and helped to stir up a wave of revival that spread across the United States. It is these young people who popularized the term *born again*.

But long before the term *born again* became so widely identified with believers, Jesus used the term in John 3:3 when He told Nicodemus, a Jewish religious leader, "Very truly I tell you, no one can see the kingdom of God unless they are born again" (John

3:3). Basically, Jesus was telling Nicodemus that "one birth is not enough."

The Need for a New Birth

Nicodemus was a seeker. But because he was a prominent Jewish leader, he didn't want people to see him talking to Jesus. So he approached Jesus at night to get answers to his questions. But even before he could begin asking questions, Jesus began speaking to the spiritual darkness of Nicodemus's heart: "Unless one is born again, he cannot see the kingdom of God" (John 3:3). Nicodemus needed a spiritual transformation that could only be produced by the Holy Spirit.

When Jesus said Nicodemus needed to be born again, initially he thought Jesus was talking about physical rebirth. Jesus then clarified what He meant: "Unless one is born of water and the Spirit, he cannot enter the kingdom of God" (verse 5). As the Bible tells us elsewhere, all people are physically born into sin and spiritual darkness. The apostle Paul painted a grim picture of man's condition when he said, "You were dead in your transgressions and sins" (Ephesians 2:1). All mankind needs a second birth!

The New Birth Defined

The spiritual transformation that is produced by the Holy Spirit is what theologians call *regeneration*. *Regeneration* is an act of God whereby eternal life is imparted to a new believer. This new birth changes a person's whole being. He is given a new heart. His mind is illuminated. His will is freed from bondage to sin. And God comes to dwell in his body.

The Nature of the New Birth

Talk about a makeover! Scripture describes this transformation in this way: "If anyone is in Christ, the new creation has come: The old has gone, the new is here!" (2 Corinthians 5:17). Read on to learn more about the miracle of the new birth.

The new birth is an act in which people are passive. No one has control over the wind. It comes and goes, and all anyone can do is feel it. Jesus said the new birth is like the wind. It comes upon a person without any effort on their part. This means no religious act you do can produce the new birth (John 3:8).

The new birth is subconscious. The new birth isn't necessarily felt, but a new believer can quickly begin to see its results. Some people may have an emotional response when regeneration occurs, but that emotional response is not proof that it has happened.

The new birth is instantaneous. Just as physical birth is immediate, so also is spiritual birth. There are no stages or steps or levels. You are either spiritually alive or not. Jesus described it this way: "Very truly I tell you, whoever hears my word and believes him who sent me has eternal life and will not be judged but has crossed over from death to life" (John 5:24).

Those Responsible for the New Birth

The author of regeneration is God the Father. In eternity past, God determined by His sovereign will to elect a people for His own possession. This election was purely by His grace and had nothing to do with any future actions by those people. However, in God's timing and by His Spirit, an act of regeneration took place with this result: "To those who believed in his name, he gave the right to become children of God" (John 1:12).

The agent of regeneration is the Holy Spirit. It is the Holy Spirit who brings about our new birth. Other scriptures call regeneration "rebirth" and "renewal" and credit the Holy Spirit as the agent of regeneration: "He saved us through the washing of rebirth and renewal by the Holy Spirit" (Titus 3:5).

The mediator of regeneration is Christ. A mediator is a go-between. Jesus, by His death and resurrection, brought reconciliation between God and sinful man, making it possible for God to enter into a relationship with man. Notice Jesus' involvement in making this new birth possible:

—"If anyone is *in Christ*, the new creation has come"
(2 Corinthians 5:17).

—"We are God's handiwork, *created in Christ Jesus*"
(Ephesians 2:10).

—"God has given us eternal life, and this *life is in his
Son*" (1 John 5:11).

—"He has given us new birth into a living hope
through the resurrection of Jesus Christ from the dead"
(1 Peter 1:3).

The instrument of regeneration is the Word. Note how Peter describes the Bible's role in the new birth: "You have been born again, not of perishable seed, but of imperishable, through the living and enduring word of God" (1 Peter 1:23).

The Evidences of the New Birth

There are obvious evidences that you are alive physically, right? Your heart is beating. You are warm to the touch. You talk. You think. And unless you are bedridden, you can move around from place to place. These are proofs that you are alive.

Similarly, there are proofs that you are alive spiritually. As the Bible says, "Examine yourselves to see whether you are in the faith; test yourselves. Do you not realize that Christ Jesus is in you—unless, of course, you fail the test?" (2 Corinthians 13:5). The book of 1 John was written for people to test and see if they are truly born again. Here are a few of the tests you can apply to your own life:

—Do you do what is right? "If you know that he is
righteous, you know that everyone who does what is
right has been born of him" (1 John 2:29).

—Do you possess the Holy Spirit? "This is how we
know that we live in him and he in us; He has given
us of his Spirit" (1 John 4:13).

—Do you believe that Jesus is God? "Everyone who believes that Jesus is the Christ is born of God, and everyone who loves the father loves his child as well" (1 John 5:1).

—Do you have victory over sin? "Everyone born of God overcomes the world. This is the victory that has overcome the world, even our faith" (1 John 5:4).

What Does This Mean for You?

Life doesn't give you "do overs," but God does. He offers you a second chance and a second birth through His Son, Jesus Christ. Have you responded to God's offer of a relationship with Him and been born again? If not, like the man Nicodemus, seek out Jesus.

If you have already experienced this new birth, then praise God and be vocal to your family and friends about the fact that "you must be born again." One birth is not enough!

34

Rescue Is Only Part of the Story

*What a wretched man I am! Who will rescue
me from this body that is subject to death?
(Romans 7:24).*

*The Lord Jesus Christ…gave himself for our sins
to rescue us from the present evil age, according
to the will of our God and Father
(Galatians 1:3-4).*

*They tell how you turned to God and…wait for his
Son from heaven, whom he raised from the dead—
Jesus, who rescues us from the coming wrath
(1 Thessalonians 1:9-10).*

We live in a world of fires, floods, earthquakes, and other kinds of disasters from which people need to be rescued. Then there are kidnappings, hostage situations, and other scenarios that require skilled rescuers as well. Some of these rescues are performed by police and fire personnel, while others are done by Navy SEALs, Special Ops teams, and other specially trained individuals.

These professionals spend a lot of time preparing for the possibility that they might need to rescue a person. Their ability to do the job well can mean the difference between a victim escaping alive or being lost.

Have you ever thought about the fact that God is in the rescue business as well? But with God, it's a different kind of rescue—He takes those who are dead and gives them life. And that is only the beginning of all that God does when He rescues someone. Let's look at what He does:

Rescue began in eternity. If you are a believer in Christ, your salvation was not a recent development on God's part. Your rescue was planned in eternity past and executed in the realm of time. Here's how it happened, as understood by the apostle Paul: "For those God foreknew he also predestined to be conformed to the image of his Son, that he might be the firstborn among many brothers and sisters. And those he predestined, he also called; those he called, he also justified; those he justified, he also glorified" (Romans 8:29-30).

God determined beforehand, in eternity past, to set His love on you and mark you out and destine you to become like Jesus, and to live with Him in eternity future.

Rescue was accomplished in time. The Bible says, "You were dead in your transgressions and sin" (Ephesians 2:1). Because you were spiritually dead, you could not comprehend your need to be rescued. You were spiritually lost and didn't know it. You didn't realize you were in grave peril. It's as if you were about to die in a burning building and don't even know it.

Unless God intervenes in the life of an unsaved person, he or she will continue down the path to eternal destruction. But thankfully, God does intervene and gives certain people—those whom He has chosen in eternity past—the desire to be rescued.

A good example of God's intervention is seen in the life of a woman named Lydia. Acts 16:14 says, "The Lord opened her heart to heed the things spoken by Paul." At God's appointed time, Lydia's eyes were opened and she realized she was in a burning building and responded to the gospel.

At a time of God's choosing, those whom He elects (Romans 8:33) see the flames and understand that unless they are rescued, they will die. Salvation is accomplished as God opens the hearts and minds of people to repent of their sins and accept Christ's death as the payment for their sins. The apostle Paul said it this way: "He has rescued us from the dominion of darkness and brought us into the kingdom of the Son he loves" (Colossians 1:13).

Rescue provides our acceptance. All unbelievers are enemies of God. But as part of God's rescue unto salvation, those who are former enemies are "accepted in the Beloved" (Ephesians 1:6 NKJV). God's grace has made it possible for sinners like you and me to be accepted as the beloved of God.

The Bible uses a variety of terms to express our acceptance by God, including *redeemed* (Romans 3:24), *reconciled* (2 Corinthians 5:19-21), *forgiven* (Romans 3:25), *justified* (Romans 3:24), and *glorified* (Romans 8:30). These declarations of acceptance are but a few of the things that result from the rescue accomplished in the life of a sinner!

Rescue procures our position. The salvation made possible by Christ has established our position before God. Nothing can separate us from being in favor with God (Romans 8:39). We are citizens of heaven (Philippians 3:20), members of a holy priesthood (1 Peter 2:5), members of the household of God (Ephesians 2:19), sons and daughters adopted into the family of God (Galatians 4:5), and God's special possessions (1 Peter 2:9). Our position in Christ was determined in eternity past, established at salvation, and secured for all eternity!

Rescue promises our inheritance. God's loving selection of you in eternity past guaranteed not only your present life but also the life to come. In God's eyes your inheritance has already been established. That's why the word "glorified" in Romans 8:30 is in the past tense. For now you are waiting for the time when you will be with God for all eternity. And as a promise of what is to come, you have been given the Holy Spirit, who "is a deposit guaranteeing [your] inheritance until the redemption of those who are God's possession" (Ephesians 1:14).

What does that inheritance look like? We are heirs of God and co-heirs with Christ (Romans 8:17). We are blessed in the heavenly realm with every spiritual blessing (Ephesians 1:3). We have an inheritance that is kept in heaven for us (1 Peter 1:4). We have a crown waiting for us—the crown of righteousness, which will be given to us by Jesus Christ (2 Timothy 4:8).

Rescue produces our enablement. One of the blessings of salvation is the power of God's presence in our lives through the indwelling Holy Spirit. The Spirit enables us to live in a way that honors Christ. When we walk by the Spirit, we will not produce the deeds of the flesh (Galatians 5:16). This enablement by God's grace frees us from the burden of sin (Romans 6:14). It makes us ministers of a new covenant, not of the law, but of the Spirit (2 Corinthians 3:6).

What Does This Mean for You?

How do people usually respond when they are rescued from a burning building, a raging flood, or a faraway wilderness? They are ecstatic! They are overjoyed, overcome with emotion, and filled with gratitude. They were lost, but have been found. They were at risk, but have been saved.

When you became a Christian, you too were rescued. You were saved from an eternity separated from God. So always remember the day of your salvation and worship the one who saved you. Out of gratitude for God's grace and mercy, you should lift up ongoing praise to God. And you should be excited about telling others who need to be rescued that Christ offers them salvation and a new life in Him.

Knowing that only God can save should prompt you to pray for unsaved family members, friends, and workmates. Ask God to open their hearts to the gospel. You are not saved for your own purposes, but to praise God, honor your Savior, and serve His people as you wait expectantly for your coming inheritance. What a glorious day that will be!

35

The Holy Spirit Is the Secret Weapon of Every Christian

You will receive power when the Holy Spirit comes on you; and you will be my witnesses in Jerusalem, and in all Judea and Samaria, and to the ends of the earth (Acts 1:8).

All of them were filled with the Holy Spirit and began to speak in other tongues as the Spirit enabled them (Acts 2:4).

Now it is God who makes both us and you stand firm in Christ. He anointed us, set his seal of ownership on us, and put his Spirit in our hearts as a deposit, guaranteeing what is to come (2 Corinthians 1:21-22).

As I read my Bible, I love to follow the lives of specific men and women and see how God transformed and used them. When the book of Acts opens, you see a small group of men and women huddled in a room in Jerusalem. But it wasn't long before this brokenhearted and defeated band of Christians were turned into a courageous force of witnesses and martyrs.

Two of my favorite people in Acts are Stephen and Philip. We meet them when they are selected by the early church to take care of the needs of the widows in Jerusalem (Acts 6:1-6). A few verses later, we see Stephen performing "great wonders and signs among the people" (verse 8). Because he had confounded the Jewish leaders in the local synagogues, he was brought before the rulers of Israel—and he powerfully admonished them for their unbelief in Christ (Acts 7:2-53).

We see similarly incredible things happen to Philip. First he is waiting on tables, and the next time we see him, he is preaching Christ in Samaria. He too was performing "signs" (Acts 8:6). What was the common denominator shared by Stephen, Philip, and the people who were together in the upper room in Jerusalem? All were "full of the Spirit." They were specially empowered to successfully accomplish God's work.

The teaching we are looking at in this chapter is that *the Holy Spirit is the secret weapon of every Christian.* This power was first given in Acts 1:8: "You will receive power when the Holy Spirit comes on you; and you will be my witnesses in Jerusalem, and in all Judea and Samaria, and to the ends of the earth." This power was given for spiritual purposes, and is uniquely connected to the ministry of the Holy Spirit.

God's power comes from the Holy Spirit. Worldly power is usually achieved by superior intellect, wealth, force, beauty, or shrewd manipulation. But the power Jesus offered to His disciples—which is also given to all believers—comes from the Holy Spirit.

In the Old Testament, God empowered only a small number of specific individuals with the Holy Spirit, such as Moses, David, and those who fashioned articles for the tabernacle and the temple. But from the time of Acts 2 onward, the Holy Spirit has come into the life of every follower of Christ, including you—and He is there to stay. This means you have His empowerment available to you for a lifetime.

God's power comes at salvation. The disciples received their power on the Day of Pentecost, when they "were filled with the Holy Spirit" (Acts 2:4). You received that same power when you put your faith and trust in Jesus Christ: "He anointed us, set his seal of ownership on us, and put his Spirit in our hearts as a deposit, guaranteeing what is to come" (2 Corinthians 1:21-22). You don't need to ask for power, or ask for more of it. At salvation, you receive all the power you will ever need.

God's power comes with obedience. When you are walking with God by His Spirit, you experience victory over the desires of the world. There's a war going on between your sinful flesh and the Spirit inside you. If you give in to the flesh and your sinful desires, then you become powerless in the fight against sin. But when you are walking in obedience to God's commands as written in the Bible, you are empowered with love, joy, peace, forbearance, kindness, goodness, faithfulness, gentleness, and self-control (Galatians 5:22-23).

God's power is available for witnessing. Jesus promised the disciples they would receive power for a specific task. He said, "You will receive power...and you will be my witnesses in Jerusalem, and in all Judea and Samaria, and to the ends of the earth." Before the coming of the Holy Spirit, His followers were timid, afraid, and disheartened. But after the coming of the Holy Spirit, their lives took a dramatic turn. They ran boldly into the streets of Jerusalem, telling anyone who would listen what they had seen and heard while they were with Jesus.

You too are empowered to be Jesus' witness. You can tell others what you have seen, heard, and learned through God's Word concerning Jesus Christ, and what you have experienced in your relationship with Him. You have...

    —conviction to speak out for Christ,

    —courage to speak up for Christ,

    —confidence to speak about Christ, and the

    —capacity to speak for Christ.

God's power helps us understand and remember the Bible. Jesus promised the disciples that the Holy Spirit would help them to remember what He had taught them. This promise was fulfilled as the disciples fanned out across the world teaching the words of Jesus. All the books of the New Testament were written either by the disciples or those closely connected to them.

Similarly, the Holy Spirit helps us as we read our Bibles. He helps us understand what we are reading, plants those truths in our minds, convinces us of God's will, and convicts us of sins we need to avoid.

God's power is for service. Christians are empowered with "spiritual gifts"—divine enablements that are to be used "for the common good" (1 Corinthians 12:7). This supernatural giftedness allows you to serve God and His people with sustained power.

On your own, you are weak and inadequate. But with God's empowerment, you can have an incredible impact, whether it's talking to a hostile crowd as Stephen did, or the energetic and far-reaching ministry demonstrated in the life of Philip.

What Does This Mean for You?

The Holy Spirit empowers obedient believers. So stay on top of things in your life. Guard against sin, and watch your words and actions. And when you slip up, be quick to make matters right with God (confess your sin) and with others (ask for forgiveness).

Rely on the indwelling power of the Holy Spirit in your life. He truly is your secret weapon. He will never leave you, and His power is fully available to you at any time...and for all times...and for all situations. When life gets tough or begins to fall apart, ask God for His help. Rely on His power in your times of trial!

36

What Is God Like? Look at Jesus

*The virgin will conceive and give birth to a
son, and they will call him Immanuel
(which means "God with us")
(Matthew 1:23).*

*In the beginning was the Word, and the Word was with
God, and the Word was God...The Word became flesh and
made his dwelling among us...No one has ever seen God,
but the one and only Son, who is himself God and is in
closest relationship with the Father, has made him known
(John 1:1,14,18).*

*I and the Father are one
(John 10:30).*

God is spirit and exists outside of time and space. His perfect holiness prevents any contact with sinful mankind. So that God could relate with His creation once again, He became a human being. Jesus, the Son of God, and equal to God in all aspects, became a man. During His life on Earth He was exposed to all the temptations humans experience, yet He never sinned. He lived a perfect life and died as an offering for the sins of mankind, and then on the third day was raised from the dead. His resurrection was proof that His sacrifice was accepted by the Father and that

He was truly the Son of God. Knowing all this and having established that Jesus is God in flesh, all we have to do is look at the life of Jesus and we will see what God is like:

God is approachable. In Jesus' day, people with the disease of leprosy were feared and considered ceremonially unclean according to Jewish law. They were outcasts from society. A leper was to yell out "Unclean, unclean!" whenever anyone approached him or passed nearby. Sadly, it was typical of people to pick up stones and throw them to drive away any leper who was begging for food nearby. In contrast, when a leper approached Jesus, He "stretched out His hand and touched him" (Mark 1:41 NKJV). How amazing! The result? The leprosy was immediately cured (verse 42).

Like the Son, God is approachable. We can talk to God 24/7. We can open our hearts in prayer and instantly, we are in His presence. It is because God is approachable that Hebrews 4:16 says, "Let us therefore come boldly to the throne of grace, that we may obtain mercy and find grace to help in time of need" (NKJV).

God is compassionate. Jesus was always ministering to the needs of the people. On one occasion a crowd followed Him into a deserted place. Rather than send them away, what did He do? "Jesus, when He came out, saw a great multitude and was moved with compassion for them." Why? "Because they were like sheep not having a shepherd." So He "began to teach them many things...[until] the day was...far spent" (Mark 6:34-35 NKJV). First He ministered to their spiritual needs, then He took care of their physical needs (verses 39-41). This is consistent with the compassion God exhibited in the Old Testament: "You are a forgiving God, gracious and compassionate, slow to anger and abounding in love" (Nehemiah 9:17).

God is faithful. Despite the distractions and the appeals of the people, Jesus remained faithful to His purpose by saying to the crowds, "I have come down from heaven not to do my will [or, by the way, the will of the crowd], but the will of him who sent me" (John 6:38). To the very end, Jesus faithfully moved toward the objective that had been set before Him by the Father. He stated His final assessment of His mission to His Father in prayer on the eve of His death: "I have brought you glory on earth by finishing the work you gave me to do" (John 17:4). And the same kind of statement was also made of God in Lamentations 3:23: "Great is your faithfulness." Jesus was faithful to fulfill His mission, and the Father is faithful as well to fulfill His many promises to His people.

God is patient. Throughout the Bible, we witness the patience of God. In one instance, God the Father was patient with His sinful creation by waiting 120 years before sending judgment in the form of a flood that destroyed all mankind from the face of the Earth except for Noah and his family (Genesis 6:3).

Jesus, as God in flesh, also reflects this same heart of patience. He was patient with His disciples and their unbelief. He was patient with all those who were genuine in their desire to know and believe in Him. Can you imagine the patience the Creator of the universe possessed to work with a group of people, His creation, even His own family, who could not grasp what He was communicating about Himself? It is this same patience that Jesus extends to you. He knows you are a work in progress!

God is loving. John, who is referred to as "the disciple whom Jesus loved" (John 13:23), gives this insight into the love Jesus had for his 12 colaborers: "When Jesus knew that His hour had come that He should depart from this world to the Father, having loved His own who were in the world, He loved them to the end" (John 13:1). Jesus also loved His friends—Martha, Mary, and Lazarus (John 11:5).

How does God show His love today? He "demonstrates His own love toward us, in that while we were yet sinners, Christ died for us" (Romans 5:8).

God is truthful. Jesus was—and is—the truth. This character quality was always on display in Jesus' life because He lived truth. He was truth. He said, "I am the way and the truth and the life" (John 14:6). And as the Master Teacher, His teaching left no chance of misunderstanding or miscommunication.

Jesus was straightforward, simple, and clear with the truth. He wanted His followers to know the truth and speak the truth. In Matthew 5:37 He said, "Let your 'Yes' be 'Yes,' and your 'No,' 'No'" (NKJV). His message was: Tell the truth! Say what you mean, and mean what you say…and do what you say you'll do or not do. Then others can trust you and believe you.

What Does This Mean for You?

Do you want to know more about God than the few qualities we've noted so far by looking at the life of Jesus? To know more about what God is like, you must first know more about His Son. A good way to do this is by reading through the four Gospels—Matthew, Mark, Luke, and John. You can then learn about the character of God by looking at the character of Jesus and how He carried out His mission on Earth. Note what the writer of Hebrews said as he described the full scope of God becoming a man—the *incarnation*:

> In the past God spoke to our ancestors through the prophets at many times and in various ways, but in these last days he has spoken to us by his Son…The Son is the radiance of God's glory and the exact representation of his being, sustaining all things by his powerful word. After he had provided purification for sins, he sat down at the right hand of the Majesty in heaven (Hebrews 1:1-3).

Knowing more about Jesus should lead you to worship Him all the more and spur within you a greater desire to mirror His character qualities in your life.

37

God Wants to Be Intimate with You

Since we have been justified through faith, we have peace with God through our Lord Jesus Christ, through whom we have gained access by faith into this grace in which we now stand (Romans 5:1-2).

His purpose was to create in himself one new humanity out of the two, thus making peace, and in one body to reconcile both of them to God through the cross, by which he put to death their hostility (Ephesians 2:15-16).

Once you were alienated from God and were enemies in your minds because of your evil behavior. But now he has reconciled you by Christ's physical body through death to present you holy in his sight, without blemish and free from accusation (Colossians 1:21-22).

Once upon a time there was a rich man who had two sons. One son was not satisfied with his role on his father's estate and longed to travel the world and experience all that life had to offer. He went to his father and asked for his share of the inheritance. With his portion of his father's riches, he left to see the world.

It wasn't long before this son squandered all his wealth. In an effort to make ends meet, the only job he could find was that of feeding pigs. In fact, he was so destitute that he found himself wanting to eat the food that was given to the pigs. Realizing his condition and recalling that his father's hired men were better off than him, the young man decided to return home. He would ask for his father's forgiveness and plead to be made one of his father's hired men.

One day while the father was keeping his daily vigil hoping for his son's return, he recognized his son a long way off in the distance. His heart was filled with compassion, and rather than wait for his son to arrive, he ran to his son and embraced him, forgiving him and restoring him to his position as a son.

You may recognize this abbreviated story as a parable told by Jesus in Luke 15:11-24. In the parable, the father represents God, who in great compassion desires to restore the intimacy between Himself and mankind that was lost when Adam and Eve fell into sin. Bible theologians will tell us that an intimate relationship with God is possible only when *reconciliation* occurs. As the parable teaches, when the rebellious son acknowledged personal responsibility for his sin, the first step toward reconciliation and restored intimacy with his father began. The Bible has much to say about reconciliation.

Reconciliation is needed. In the beginning there was an intimate relationship between God and His human creations. But as soon as man sinned, that relationship was broken. We read in Genesis 3:8 that when Adam and Eve "heard the sound of the LORD God walking in the garden in the cool of the day...[they] hid themselves from the presence of the LORD God." That indicates to us that up to that point, God desired to interact with His creation— that's why He was "in the garden." But because of sin, man was now afraid of a relationship with God. Adam told God, "I was afraid because I was naked and I hid myself."

From this point onward, sinful man was alienated from a holy God. If God had not intervened, man would have continued on in rebellion and estrangement from his Creator. God took the first step, and "while we were still sinners, Christ died for us" (Romans 5:8).

Reconciliation means restoration. Reconciliation means restoring a relationship. In the biblical sense, it is the restoration of fellowship between God and man. It involves the removal of sin, which changes the relationship between God and man from one of hostility to one of friendship. Without reconciliation, there can be no relationship.

Reconciliation's objects are both God and man. Reconciliation involves both God and man. It changes the relationship between the two parties, who are no longer separated by the barrier of sin. Here's how both parties are involved:

> Man is the object of reconciliation—God effects a change in man through the removal of sin by the death of Christ, therefore restoring the harmony between God and man. Paul affirms man as the object of reconciliation in 2 Corinthians 5:18-19, where he says, "All this is from God, who *reconciled us to himself* through Christ...that God was *reconciling the world to himself in Christ, not counting people's sins against them.*"
>
> God is the object of reconciliation—Reconciliation is the removal of the hostility or wrath from the alienated parties. Therefore, the death of Christ removed God's enmity against man. Once again, but from the opposite direction, the apostle Paul affirms that God is also the object of reconciliation in Romans 5:10: "While we were God's enemies, *we were reconciled to him* through the death of his Son."

Reconciliation was accomplished at Calvary. Calvary signifies the location of the cross on which Christ died. Christ's death accomplished both universal and individual reconciliation. The Bible says that "God reconciled the world to Himself" with Christ's payment for sin on the cross. Because sin's debt was paid, the way is now clear for people to be reconciled to God.

The fact of reconciliation does not mean that everyone in the world will desire or receive that reconciliation. It is not realized until a person turns to God. That's why Paul urges, "Be reconciled to God" (2 Corinthians 5:20). Reconciliation is offered through Christ's death, but it occurs only when a person receives God's forgiveness in Christ, as this verse affirms: "We also rejoice in God through our Lord Jesus Christ, through whom we have now received the reconciliation" (Romans 5:11 NKJV).

What Does This Mean for You?

The news that God and man can be reconciled is the central message of the gospel. The war between God and man is over. If you have received Jesus Christ as Lord and Savior, your sins are blotted out and you have been made righteous. You are no longer God's enemy, or a stranger or foreigner to Him.

This is great news—news worthy of sharing with others. Because you have been reconciled, God "has committed to [you] the message of reconciliation" (2 Corinthians 5:19). As such, you "are therefore Christ's ambassadors, as though God were making his appeal through [you]. We implore you on Christ's behalf: Be reconciled to God" (verse 20). Do you need to convey this message of reconciliation to someone today?

Because of the reconciliation that comes through Christ, you are at peace with God and have been given personal access to Him through His Son, Jesus Christ (Hebrews 10:22). You can talk to God anytime, day or night, 365 days a year because of your intimate relationship. He hears your prayers and personalizes His responses for you according to His will. Because of your kinship to God, you can know that His actions on your behalf will always be in your best interests.

38

The Lord Is My Shepherd

The LORD is my shepherd, I lack nothing. He makes me lie down in green pastures, he leads me beside quiet waters, he refreshes my soul (Psalm 23:1-2).

I am the good shepherd. The good shepherd lays down his life for the sheep (John 10:11).

My sheep listen to my voice; I know them, and they follow me. I give them eternal life, and they shall never perish; no one will snatch them out of my hand (John 10:27-28).

I'll never forget the day I rounded a curve on a back country road and almost ran right into a flock of sheep and a shepherd, complete with a sheep dog! I couldn't believe my eyes because I was in Ventura County, just north of the metropolis of Los Angeles.

Yes, sheep and shepherds still exist in this modern-day world. And yet the idea of shepherding is a foreign concept for most people, especially those of us who live in cities. You don't come across many shepherds hanging out in Times Square in New York City, or grazing their flocks in Pershing Square in downtown Los Angeles.

And for sure you won't see many shepherds leading their flocks down the Magnificent Mile in Chicago.

But shepherds and sheep are very much a part of biblical culture. Shepherds fulfilled a vital function for the agrarian people of Bible times, and that hasn't changed much over time. Even today in the Middle East herds of sheep and shepherds can be seen everywhere, doing what they have done for thousands of years. And the everyday functions of shepherds and sheep illustrate very well for us the ways that Christ, the Great Shepherd, cares for us, His sheep.

Christ sacrificed Himself for His sheep. A shepherd's job is to protect his sheep. A good shepherd will not run away when savage wolves threaten the flock. Jesus willingly sacrificed Himself so His sheep could have eternal life.

Christ provides security for His sheep. In the same way that sheep are vulnerable to physical attack, God's people are constantly at risk when it comes to spiritual attack. We need protection. Jesus promised those who follow Him that none of the forces of evil would be able to snatch them out of His hand, and that the new life they have in Him will last forever (John 10:28). With Jesus as our Shepherd, we are in safe hands. We have nothing to fear.

Christ does not leave His sheep without help. Jesus is no longer on Earth, so how is He able to give His followers help, assistance, and direction? As the Good Shepherd, Jesus has given us the gift of His Spirit to live in us (John 14:17) and act as our helper and teacher (verse 26) in His absence.

But Jesus has also given us another gift—spiritual leaders who can teach and guide us: "So Christ himself gave the apostles, the prophets, the evangelists, the pastors and teachers, to equip his people for works of service, so that the body of Christ may be built up" (Ephesians 4:11-12).

Christ provides leadership for His sheep. The very title of *shepherd* implies leadership. The sheep follow their leader, as described in Psalm 23:2: "He leads me beside quiet waters." Jesus is the ultimate Shepherd, and therefore the ultimate leader: "And God placed all things under his feet and appointed him to be head over everything for the church, which is his body, the fullness of him who fills everything in every way" (Ephesians 1:22-23).

As our leader, Jesus expects His followers to:

—live in absolute obedience to Him,

—imitate His life before a watching world,

—use their spiritual gifts in His service, and

—adopt a servant's heart.

Christ intercedes in behalf of His sheep. As a shepherd looks out for the interests of his sheep, so Jesus looks after His people's interests and intercedes for them. Jesus makes perpetual intercession before God for us. His continuous presence in heaven with the Father assures us that our sins have been paid for and forgiven: "He is able to save completely those who come to God through him, because he always lives to intercede for them" (Hebrews 7:25).

Christ is our advocate before the Father. Human beings are separated from God by sin. Only one person in the universe can be our advocate, our mediator. Only one person can stand between us and God and bring us back into a right relationship—Jesus, who is both God and man. Jesus presents His righteousness to the Father for our justification. The apostle Paul describes how Jesus represents us before God the Father with these words: "There is one God and one mediator between God and mankind, the man Christ Jesus, who gave himself as a ransom for all people" (1 Timothy 2:5-6).

Christ is coming again. While on Earth, Jesus spoke of Himself as the "good shepherd" (John 10:11). He said His sheep would know and respond to His voice and follow Him (verses 3-4). Though Jesus is presently in heaven, there is coming a day when He will return for His sheep. He told His disciples, "If I go and prepare a place for you, I will come back and take you to be with me that you also may be where I am" (John 14:3).

What Does This Mean for You?

Back when Jesus ministered here on Earth, He came as a lowly shepherd. But when He returns, He will come as a judge: "I saw heaven standing open and there before me was a white horse, whose rider is called Faithful and True. With justice he judges and wages war" (Revelation 19:11).

In the meantime, you must ask these two questions: Does Jesus know me as one of His sheep? Will I know His voice when He calls His sheep? If you cannot answer these questions with a resounding *yes*, you need to ask Jesus to come into your life and become your Savior and your "good shepherd."

And if you are one of His sheep, what should you be doing? The awareness that no one knows the day Christ will return should motivate you to always be prepared. You are to live responsibly, avoiding a life of self-serving pleasure. You are to humbly serve others in Christ's body, the church, doing your part in the work of building God's kingdom. You are to make every moment count in light of the fact Jesus could return at any time.

39

Turn or Burn

*He will say to those on his left, "Depart from
me, you who are cursed, into the eternal fire
prepared for the devil and his angels"
(Matthew 25:41).*

*Anyone whose name was not found written in the
book of life was thrown into the lake of fire
(Revelation 20:15).*

There are some religions that speak of a terrible place of punishment where evil people go when they die. The reason they
are sent there is because they did not believe in a particular god,
or they didn't correctly practice the god's rituals, or are in some
way not seen as worthy. This place has many names, but in the
Bible, it is known as hell. Scripture teaches that hell is a literal place
of anguish and suffering produced by an eternal fire prepared for
those who are wicked.

The only hope for anyone who wants to avoid this awful place
is, as the title of this chapter says, "Turn or burn." A person needs
to turn from his wicked ways, or burn in hell for eternity. Let's
look to the Bible now and see what it says about hell and eternal
punishment.

The Bible Uses Different Terms to Speak of Eternal Punishment

Eternal punishment takes place in hell, also referred to as "the lake of fire" or "Gehenna." The Bible uses three words to describe this place: (1) Sheol, or "grave," is used in the Old Testament to mean the place of the dead, generally thought to be under the Earth—"the grave snatches away those who have sinned" (Job 24:19). (2) *Hades* is a Greek term that refers to the underworld and the place of the dead—"and death and Hades gave up the dead" (Revelation 20:13). (3) Gehenna, in Jesus' day, was an actual place nearby Jerusalem where the people would dump and burn their trash. The fires there burned continually.

Jesus Taught About Hell

Jesus often taught on the subject of hell—so much so that it's clearly an important topic. Here are several of Jesus' descriptions of hell:

—A place so severe it would be better to cut off a hand or lose an eye if it leads to going to hell (Matthew 5:29-30).

—A place for the ungodly away from the presence of Christ (Matthew 7:23).

—A place of ultimate punishment where there will be "weeping and gnashing of teeth" (Matthew 8:12).

—A place worse than death, "where the fire never goes out" (Mark 9:43).

—A place of outer darkness (Matthew 22:13).

Based on Jesus' teachings, we can only conclude that hell is a terrible reality.

The Apostles Taught About Hell

The apostles followed Christ in teaching that there are only two ultimate destinations for people—eternal bliss, or the torment of hell.

Paul—He wrote of the impending judgment of God, saying that for those "who reject the truth and follow evil, there will be wrath and anger. There will be trouble and distress for every human being who does evil" (Romans 2:8-9). These evildoers will appear at the Great White Throne judgment (Revelation 19:11-15).

Peter—He referred to God's punishment of fallen angels when he said, "God did not spare angels when they sinned, but sent them to hell, putting them in chains of darkness to be held for judgment" (2 Peter 2:4). The ungodly who revel in sin will be destroyed in the same destruction" (verse 12). The "blackest darkness" is reserved for evildoers (verse 17).

John—He described both the place and people who will inhabit hell. In Revelation 14:11, he said hell is a place where "the smoke of their torment will rise for ever and ever. There will be no rest day or night." In Revelation 21:8, he said that all unbelievers "will be consigned to the fiery lake of burning sulfur. This is the second death."

There Is No Second Chance in Hell

The Bible teaches there is no second chance after death: "People are destined to die once, and after that to face judgment" (Hebrews 9:27). The book of Revelation states clearly that "death and the grave [will be] thrown into the lake of fire" (20:14). The lake of fire is the ultimate destination of everything wicked—Satan, the beast, the false prophet, the demons, death, hades, and all those whose names are not recorded in the book of life because they did not place their faith in Jesus Christ. There is no hope, no second chance, no other appeal for heaven and being with God when a person dies without putting their faith in Christ.

The Punishment of Hell Is Just

The Bible says, "The heavens declare the glory of God; the skies proclaim the work of his hands" (Psalm 19:1). God has revealed Himself plainly in His creation to all people. And yet people reject even this basic knowledge of God.

God has also "set eternity in the human heart" (Ecclesiastes 3:11). Everyone has an inner sense of God and what He requires, but they choose not to live by it. Because of their rejection of God, they will inevitably face His wrath: "The wrath of God is being revealed from heaven against all the godlessness and wickedness of people, who suppress the truth by their wickedness" (Romans 1:18). It all comes down to the nature of God ("The LORD is known by his acts of justice") and the nature of man ("the wicked are ensnared by the work of their hands") (Psalm 9:16).

"Turn or Burn?"

The reality of hell is difficult for some people to resolve in their minds, especially those who don't believe in God. So they procrastinate when it comes to learning more about it or about their need for salvation. They say, "Someday I'll think about it," or "Someday I'll make a decision one way or the other." But to keep God at arm's length is actually a decision against God and salvation. There is no middle ground—either a person is saved, or he isn't.

There are some people who ask, "If God is truly loving, how could He send anyone to hell?" But to ask that is to ignore God's justice. He is not only a God of love, but also a God of justice. Because He cannot tolerate sin, He must banish it from His presence. It is in love that He offers the gift of salvation available through Jesus Christ, and it is in justice that He will one day restore all righteousness and punish those who don't want to have anything to do with Him. As 2 Peter 3:9 says, it is not God's choice for "anyone to perish, but [for] everyone to come to repentance" (2 Peter 3:9). It is not God, but man's own choice that earns him eternity in hell.

What Does This Mean for You?

In the Christian life, as we stay active serving God, loving one another, and getting involved in our church, it's easy to forget that at one time, we were lost sinners destined for hell. So each time we are reminded by the Bible of hell, we need to give thanks to God not only for our salvation, but also for the fact that we have been delivered from condemnation and eternal suffering in hell.

What's more, the reality and severity of hell should compel you to speak out to those who have not yet received Christ as Savior. Hell is for real, a place you would not wish upon anyone, even your worst enemy. Jesus warned others repeatedly about hell, and so should you! Let them know what Jesus said:

> I will show you whom you should fear:
> Fear him who, after your body has been killed,
> has authority to throw you into hell.
> Yes, I tell you, fear him (Luke 12:5).

40

How Much Water Is Enough?

*Go and make disciples of all nations, baptizing them in the
name of the Father and of the Son and of the Holy Spirit
(Matthew 28:19).*

*"Sirs, what must I do to be saved?" They replied,
"Believe in the Lord Jesus, and you will be saved—
you and your household."...then immediately
he and all his household were baptized
(Acts 16:30-33).*

Some time ago, my wife and I, along with family and friends,
watched two of our grandchildren get baptized in the great
expanse of the Pacific Ocean. In a sense, then, I guess you could
say it took the entire ocean for two teens to fulfill our Lord Jesus'
command to be baptized. The point, however, is they were baptized
by immersion—that is, they were lowered to the point they were
fully covered by water, then raised up again. But I have also talked
to people who said that as an infant or later in their life, a priest or
minister had taken a small cup or handful of water and sprinkled
them with it, thus constituting their baptism.

Exactly when should baptism take place? And exactly and how
much water is required to fulfill Jesus' command to baptize a person

"in the name of the Father and of the Son and of the Holy Spirit" (Matthew 28:19)? Baptism is an important ordinance in the Bible and a teaching worthy of our attention.

Baptism Was a Jewish Practice

Early in the New Testament we are introduced to John the Baptist, who baptized and preached a baptism of repentance for the remission of sins (Mark 1:4). He was baptizing people to symbolically prepare them for the arrival of the Messiah.

Baptism's New Testament Meaning

The baptism commanded of all Christians is symbolic as well, and is not a step in the process of salvation. Because baptism is so often spoken of in connection with the act of repentance, there are some who teach that it's a required part of becoming a Christian. But when the apostle Peter said, "Repent and be baptized…in the name of Jesus Christ for the forgiveness of your sins" (Acts 2:38), he wasn't teaching that baptism was a part of one's salvation. Rather, he was affirming the symbolic nature of baptism. That's evident by his comparison of baptism to the ark and the salvation of Noah and his family: "In [the ark] only a few people, eight in all, were saved through water, and this water symbolizes baptism that now saves you also—not the removal of dirt from the body but the pledge of a clear conscience toward God. It saves you by the resurrection of Jesus Christ" (1 Peter 3:20-21). Salvation, according to Peter, was not by the water but by "the pledge of a clear conscience toward God."

Why Should One Be Baptized?

If baptism doesn't save, then you might be thinking, *why is it necessary?* Here are two reasons:

The Lord's command—"Go and make disciples of all nations, baptizing them" (Matthew 28:19). The word of our Lord is a sufficient reason for a believer to be baptized. No further authority is needed. Baptism then should be the first act of obedience after becoming a Christian.

The practice of the early church—The apostles were aware of Jesus' command concerning baptism. Therefore, at the birth of the church on the Day of Pentecost, after a large multitude of people became saved upon hearing Peter's sermon about Christ, "those who gladly received his word were baptized" (Acts 2:41). There was never any doubt that baptism was to *follow* repentance, and not be part of the act of repentance.

Who Should Be Baptized?

What are the three qualifications that must be met before one is baptized?

1. Disciples—Jesus said, "Go make *disciples*" (Matthew 28:19). To be baptized, one must be a disciple—a follower of Jesus Christ. A disciple is one who identifies with his teacher and understands the teacher's teaching.

2. Believers—"Those who gladly received his word were baptized" (Acts 2:41). Later, in Acts 8, an Ethiopian eunuch confessed his faith in Jesus as the son of God, and he was baptized (verses 36-38). After the Philippian jailer and his family became saved, he "and all his household were baptized...he was filled with joy because *he had come to believe in God*—he and his whole household" (Acts 16:33-34).

3. Those who have received the Holy Spirit—Peter was privileged to preach the gospel, first to the Jews in Acts 2, and later in Acts 10 to the Gentiles at the home of a centurion named Cornelius. "While Peter was still speaking these words, the Holy Spirit came on all who heard the message...Then Peter said, 'Surely no one can stand in the way of their being baptized with water. *They have received the Holy Spirit* just as we have.' So he ordered that they be baptized in the name of Jesus Christ" (verses 44-48).

The Symbolism of Baptism

To review, baptism symbolizes a person's identification with Jesus. In Romans 6:3-4, Paul gave a graphic picture of how believers identify with Christ:

> Death: "Don't you know that all of us who were baptized into Christ Jesus were baptized into his death?" (verse 3).

> Burial: "We were therefore buried with him through baptism into death" (verse 4).

> Resurrection: "…in order that, just as Christ was raised from the dead through the glory of the Father, we too may live a new life" (verse 4).

Romans 6:3-4 is not referring to water baptism, but to the spiritual symbolism behind the physical act of water baptism and a person's identification with Christ.

Now, baptism is more than a declaration of identification with Christ in His death, burial, and resurrection. It is also an acknowledgment that the old self and his ways are dead: "We know that our old self was crucified with him so that the body ruled by sin might be done away with, that we should no longer be slaves to sin" (Romans 6:6).

How Should We Baptize?

The original New Testament Greek word translated "baptize" means "to dip or immerse." However, around the time when the Bible was translated into English, sprinkling was the accepted practice by the Church of England. So, rather than offend anyone, the Greek word *baptizo* was introduced into the English Bible as "baptism" without defining its meaning. But in Romans 6:3-4, the apostle Paul clearly described baptism by immersion—we are "buried with him through baptism into death." That symbolism is lost in the practice of sprinkling. Furthermore, all the other examples of baptism recorded in Scripture imply immersion rather than sprinkling (see, for example, Matthew 3:16 and Mark 2:9-10).

What Does This Mean for You?

If or when you are baptized, you are making a public profession of your identification with Christ, your commitment to walk in newness of life, and your desire to renounce your old life, in which you served sin and Satan. You are declaring that you are on the path of righteousness and in the service of Christ. If you are reading these words as one who has trusted in Christ but has not yet been baptized, let me urge upon you the importance of obedience to Christ Himself. How can you neglect a command that came from your Savior and God?

And, how much water is enough? Enough to clearly picture that you are identifying with Christ's death, burial, and resurrection. The Pacific Ocean fulfilled this requirement very nicely for my grandchildren!

41

Membership Has Its Privileges

His intent was that now, through the church, the manifold wisdom of God should be made known to the rulers and authorities in the heavenly realms (Ephesians 3:10).

As you come to him, the living Stone—rejected by humans but chosen by God and precious to him—you also, like living stones, are being built into a spiritual house to be a holy priesthood (1 Peter 2:4-5).

Let us not neglect our meeting together, as some people do, but encourage one another, especially now that the day of his return is drawing near (Hebrews 10:25 NLT).

Anyone who likes living or being alone is usually seen as eccentric, peculiar, or odd. It's hard to imagine anyone not being a member of some group, organization, or club, either for business or pleasure. Typically an organization or club has standards that members are expected to follow. So the idea of membership, or belonging to some group or organization, is a well-known concept.

If you are a believer in Jesus Christ, whether you realize it or not, you are a member of Christ's body, the church. Your membership was instituted the moment you became a believer. And what exactly is the church? Just as the nation of Israel was God's instrument for proclaiming His name and demonstrating His grace and mercy in the Old Testament, the church is God's instrument in the New Testament era and the current age. To understand more about the church, here are a few biblical facts from just one book of the New Testament, Ephesians:

Christ is the head of the church (Ephesians 1:22).

The church is Christ's body (1:23).

The church is to show forth the wisdom of God (3:10).

The church is subject to Christ (5:24).

Christ loved and died for the church (5:25).

Christ feeds and cares for His church (5:29).

Believers are members of Christ's body, the church (5:30).

Membership in Christ's church gives believers incredible privileges, but this membership also comes with many responsibilities.

The privileges of membership. In Ephesians 1, Paul wrote about the blessings of being a part of the church:

You were chosen before the foundation of time (verse 4).

You were adopted as a son (verse 5).

You were forgiven of sin (verse 7).

You have been given an inheritance (verse 11).

You were sealed in Christ by the Holy Spirit (verse 13).

The responsibilities of membership. Privilege always comes with responsibility, and membership in the body of Christ has its obligations. In Ephesians 4, God asks believers to fulfill their "membership duties":

You are to live a life worthy of your calling (verse 1).

You are to be patient with others in love (verse 2).

You are to be trained by your church leaders for works
of service (verse 12).

You are to become spiritually mature (verse 13).

The goal of membership. When a person becomes a Christian, he
doesn't understand all the ramifications of his new life in Christ.
All he knows is that once he was spiritually blind, and now he sees.
Now he must "grow in the grace and knowledge of our Lord and
Savior Jesus Christ" (2 Peter 3:18).

Jesus has a plan and purpose for each believer—that "we all
reach unity in the faith and in the knowledge of the Son of God
and become mature, attaining to the whole measure of the fullness
of Christ" (Ephesians 4:13). This goal must be the lifelong passion
of every member of the body of Christ. And Christ, knowing our
weaknesses, has given believers an incredible resource in the Holy
Spirit.

The empowerment of membership. When a person accepts Jesus
Christ as Savior, the Spirit of Jesus (Philippians 1:19) comes to live
in that new believer and provides what are called *spiritual gifts.* A
spiritual gift is a spiritual ability given by God and empowered
by the Holy Spirit for the purpose of ministering to others in the
body of Christ.

Three passages are key to understanding the importance and
significance of spiritual gifts: Romans 12:4-8, 1 Corinthians 12:1-31,
and 1 Peter 4:10-11. Here are some basic principles these passages
teach us about spiritual gifts.

They are given at salvation.

They are not natural abilities.

They are not to be distinguished as greater or lesser.

They are not to be a source of pride.

They are for the benefit of other believers.

They are used in the presence of other believers.

The conditions of membership. Every organization has its code of ethics or rules for staying in "good graces" with the organization. Christ has only one condition for staying in good standing: *obedience.* He said, "If you love me, keep my commands" (John 14:15).

Jesus also said, "Take my yoke upon you and learn from me...For my yoke is easy and my burden is light" (Matthew 11:29-30). Jesus lovingly demands that His followers obey His commands as stated in His Word, the Bible. This isn't impossible for us to do, for His "burden is light." He has also given the members of His body men who are especially gifted to lead His people (Ephesians 4:11-12). Jesus asks these leaders to watch over His people and requires that His followers obey them as they would obey Him: "Have confidence in your leaders and submit to their authority, because they keep watch over you as those who must give an account" (Hebrews 13:17).

What Does This Mean for You?

Membership in the body of Christ is the greatest of all memberships, and the privileges are exceptional both in this life and the life to come. Hopefully you are already actively involved in your local church. If not, let the command of Hebrews 10:25 be a reminder of your need to do this: "Let us not neglect our meeting together, as some people do, but encourage one another, especially now that the day of his return is drawing near" (Hebrews 10:25 NLT).

Church is important to God and His Son, Jesus. You and your fellow believers are "living stones, [and] are being built into a spiritual house to be a holy priesthood" (1 Peter 2:5). You can demonstrate that the church is important in your life in these ways:

Attend faithfully—Worshipping God and growing spiritually should be key priorities in your life. Obviously you can worship God anywhere and at any time, but worship is not just an

individual experience, but a collective one as well. And as you worship God with other Christians, you'll also have the opportunity
to develop and use your spiritual gifts.

Give generously—It is said that you can tell what a person's priorities are by looking at their checkbook or credit card statement.
When you invest your "treasure" in God's church and God's people,
you have a much greater "heart" interest in the well-being of others. Why? Because "where your treasure is, there your heart will be
also" (Matthew 6:21).

Pray regularly—The apostle Paul often asked his readers to
"pray in the Spirit on all occasions with all kinds of prayers and
requests. With this in mind, be alert and always keep on praying
for all the saints" (Ephesians 6:18). As a member of Christ's body,
you should pray regularly not only for your family, but also for your
church family, its leaders, and its ministries. Create a prayer list for
the people you know both in and out of the church, and then "pray
continually" (1 Thessalonians 5:17).

Serve diligently—Whatever spiritual gifts you possess as a
member of Christ's body, you are to follow Christ's example of
serving others. Jesus said that "the Son of Man did not come to be
served, but to serve" (Matthew 20:28). Serving others can begin
right after a person receives Christ, and a key reason for serving is
that when you serve others, you are serving the Lord Jesus Christ
(Colossians 3:24).

42

Jesus Brings a Different Kind of Happiness

This day is holy to our Lord. Do not grieve, for the joy of the LORD is your strength (Nehemiah 8:10).

You became imitators of us and of the Lord, for you welcomed the message in the midst of severe suffering with the joy given by the Holy Spirit (1 Thessalonians 1:6).

Consider it pure joy, my brothers and sisters, whenever you face trials of many kinds (James 1:2).

As a human being, you possess the essence of your parents and ancestors in your DNA. When you accept Jesus as your Lord and Savior, you become a new creation who is indwelt by the Holy Spirit, all of which was made possible by your union with the Son. God's gift is described as "the Spirit of Jesus" (Philippians 1:19), or the Holy Spirit.

This great gift of the Holy Spirit gives you the ability to live a godly life. The Holy Spirit gives you all the spiritual resources you need to live God's way. The resources are there, but at the same time, you are still commanded to "walk by the Spirit…[so] you will not gratify the desires of the flesh" (Galatians 5:16). The result of your "walk by the Spirit," or your moment-by-moment submission to the Spirit's leading, will exhibit "the fruit of the Spirit." Among the fruit of the Spirit is joy—and it's important that we understand this joy is not the same thing as happiness.

Happiness Is Not Joy

When life is good, things are going well, and problems are few, praise and thanksgiving flow freely from our hearts and lips. When the sun is shining brightly, we are *happy*. But when life turns dark and stormy, praise and thanksgiving don't flow quite so easily. When our circumstances go downhill, our mood changes to one of being *unhappy*.

There is a big difference between spiritual joy and the emotion of happiness. Happiness is an emotion that we experience when we've had good fortune and success. Spiritual joy, by contrast, is a deep, inner fulfillment that manages to stay positive and God-focused even when things go wrong. The fact we can experience joy in the midst of difficulties is made evident by James 1:2, which says we are to "consider it pure joy…whenever you face trials of many kinds."

Happiness will normally cave in when trials arrive, but spiritual joy perseveres even when life gets difficult. It sacrifices the urge to give in to depression or anger. The Spirit's joy causes Christians to "in everything give thanks; for this is the will of God in Christ Jesus for you" (1 Thessalonians 5:18 NKJV). This is why one accurate definition of joy is "the sacrifice of praise."

Divine Exchange

Although you don't always feel like praising the Lord or thanking Him, you choose to do what God says, and in spite of your circumstances, make the effort to have joy. That's why it's a "sacrifice."

In James 1:2, we are told to "consider" or "count" our trials as "joy." In other words, we are to respond to negative circumstances not with anger or frustration, but with joy. The decision is ours, but the strength to follow through and live out the Spirit's joy comes from the power of the Holy Spirit. When we would rather bask in self-pity or stay stuck in depression, we choose, by divine exchange, to look beyond our pain and make the sacrifice of praise to God.

Examples of Spiritual Joy

Jesus Himself gives us the supreme model of joy in the midst of life's dark pain. There was probably no greater source of pain in the ancient world than crucifixion on a Roman cross. Yet we read in Hebrews 12:2, "For the joy set before him he endured the cross, scorning its shame." Knowing that His suffering would result in great joy, Jesus willingly endured the excruciating pain of death on the cross. He looked past the cross to His return to the Father and to eternity with all who belong to Him. And the same incredible joy Jesus experienced in His darkest hour is available to believers today!

The apostles also provide us with strong examples of joy in persecution. After they received the Holy Spirit on the Day of Pentecost (Acts 2:1-4), they immediately began to preach the resurrection of Jesus. As a result, they were brought before the religious leaders in Jerusalem and warned to stop speaking about Jesus...or else! They were threatened and beaten, which usually meant a flogging of 39 lashes. How did the disciples respond? "They departed from the presence of the council, rejoicing that they were counted worthy to suffer shame for His name" (Acts 5:41 NKJV). Theirs was definitely a "sacrifice of praise"!

What Does This Mean for You?

Jesus said, "In this world you will have trouble" (John 16:33). The question is not *if,* but *when* you will be hit with a trial or experience some sort of suffering. When that happens, let it drive you toward God. Let your trial compel you to offer Him a sacrifice of praise. Yes, Jesus said, "You will have trouble," but He also went on to say in that same verse, "But take heart! I have overcome the world."

As a result of Christ's victory on the cross and your new birth in Him, you are able to drink deeply from God's unending stream of joy—regardless of what life brings your way.

Remember:

> —Joy is not dependent on circumstances, but on the spiritual realities of God's goodness, which includes His unconditional love for you.

> —Joy is not based on your efforts, accomplishments, or willpower, but rather on the truth about your relationship with the Father through His Son.

> —Joy is not merely an emotion, but the result of choosing to look beyond what appears to be true in your life to what is true about your life in Christ.

God has done all this for you. Your part in experiencing the joy of the Spirit is to cultivate spiritual joy in your daily walk with God. How? Each day, purpose to…

> —Walk by the Spirit. This means keeping a short record with God. When you sin, quickly confess it and reestablish your dependence upon Jesus. Then when a trial comes, you are already "in the Spirit" and ready to respond with joy.

> —Offer the sacrifice of praise to God continually, even when you don't feel like it. Through the power of the Holy Spirit, this act of thanksgiving transforms your pain into praise.

> —Choose to let your trials become the soil out of which joy will blossom and grow. This happens when you let life's hard times drive you nearer to the Lord, the only source of genuine joy and real hope.

—Give thanks in everything. Whatever is happening—
good or bad—give thanks to God for His sovereignty, His purpose, His perfect timing, His perfect
plan, and His unconditional love.

—Obey God's command to be joyful. Joy is an act of
the will; it comes from making a deliberate choice
to rejoice always (Philippians 4:4). Don't sit around
waiting for joy to "just happen." Pursue it in your
every circumstance.

*Gracious Father, I pray I will walk out the door of my
home today filled with the Spirit's joy. In spite of what
happens this day, I pray that an attitude of joy will
always be evident in me, and that I will reflect the joy of
Christ, my Savior. Amen.*

43

Angels Are Not Just Something You Put on the Top of Your Christmas Tree

Do you think I cannot call on my Father, and he will at once put at my disposal more than twelve legions of angels? (Matthew 26:53).

I looked and heard the voice of many angels, numbering thousands upon thousands, and ten thousand times ten thousand. They encircled the throne and the living creatures and the elders (Revelation 5:11).

The devil, who deceived them, was thrown into the lake of burning sulfur, where the beast and the false prophet had been thrown. They will be tormented day and night for ever and ever (Revelation 20:10).

If you are like many people, when you think of angels, your mind immediately thinks about the figure many people place on the top of a Christmas tree. Perhaps we are inclined to respond this way because the Christmas story in Luke 2 mentions angels who spoke to the shepherds. The only problem is that, as far as we can tell, none of the angels who visited Earth had wings. For example, the angel at Jesus' tomb had an appearance "like lightning, and his clothes were white as snow," but no mention is made of wings (Matthew 28:3).

The English word *angel* comes from the Greek word *angelos*, meaning "messenger." So in Scripture, an angel is essentially a created being whose task is to be a messenger from God. We are also able to determine from Scripture that angels possess powers that humans don't. And when they appear, they do so in human form. In addition, they execute God's will (Psalm 103:20), they stand in God's presence and worship Him (Psalm 29:1-2), and they will accompany Christ at His second coming (Matthew 25:31).

Only two angels are mentioned by name in Scripture—Gabriel, who delivered a message to Zechariah about the birth of John the Baptist and another message to Mary about the birth of Jesus; and Michael the archangel, or "one of the chief princes" (Daniel 10:13).

Angels Fall into Two Categories—Good and Bad

Good angels. This category is made up of holy angels or angels of God. Jesus also spoke of "his angels" as those who could be called upon to provide assistance (Matthew 24:31). Michael is described as the commander of the army of good angels who defeated and expelled the bad angels from heaven (Revelation 12:7-8). Gabriel, the other good angel named in the Bible, appears to be the chief messenger angel.

Even within the category of good angels there are different kinds of angels:

> Cherubim—The first kind of angels mentioned in the Bible are cherubim (plural of *cherub*). They were celestial beings sent by God to guard the tree of life in the Garden of Eden (Genesis 3:24). They were represented symbolically on the ark of the covenant (Exodus 25:18-22), in the tabernacle (Exodus 26:31) and temple (2 Chronicles 3:7), and seen by the

prophet Ezekiel in a vision of the restored Jerusalem (Ezekiel 41:18-20).

Seraphim—These angels have their ministry in heaven. They were seen by Isaiah in a vision as hovering above the throne of God and described as having six wings: With two wings they covered their faces, with two they covered their feet, and with two they flew (Isaiah 6:1-3).

Guardian angels—These are sent by God to minister to all believers (Hebrews 1:14), and to those angels who guide the affairs of nations, also called "the chief princes" (Daniel 10:10-14).

Rulers and authorities—These terms are used by Paul to describe different orders of angels, but their specific functions are unclear (Ephesians 1:21 NASB).

God's messengers—These good angels announced and heralded the birth of Christ. They also tended to Jesus in the wilderness and in the Garden of Gethsemane. They were present at the empty tomb of the resurrected Lord and at His ascension into heaven. In the future they will proclaim God's messages of judgment (Revelation 14–17) and, as messengers, will execute God's judgments (Revelation 20:1-3).

Bad angels. This category of angelic beings consists of "the devil and his angels" (Matthew 25:41). They formerly resided in heaven, but they were unfaithful to God and were driven out of heaven and cast down to Earth by the holy angels. Satan is the chief advocate of evil and wickedness in this group of fallen angels. The Bible describes Satan (also called the devil) a number of different ways:

The anointed cherub (Ezekiel 28:14)

The prince of demons (Luke 11:15)

The god of this age (2 Corinthians 4:4)

The ruler of the kingdom of the air (Ephesians 2:2)

The prince of this world (John 14:30)

Beelzebub, the prince of demons (Matthew 12:24)

A devouring lion (1 Peter 5:8)

Satan and his fallen angels have quite a devious agenda:

To oppose God's work (Zechariah 3:1)

To pervert God's Word (Matthew 4:6)

To hinder God's workers (1 Thessalonians 2:18)

To entrap God's people (1 Timothy 3:7)

To overpower God's children (1 Peter 5:8)

To hold the world in their power (1 John 5:19)

Although Satan as an angel is very powerful, he does not possess the ability to be in more than one place at a time. But with the many demons who do his bidding, it may seem like he is everywhere.

Satan is also not all-knowing, and he cannot read minds. He does, however, manipulate people into doing his bidding. That's exactly what he did with Eve in the garden.

The angel Satan is evil and the father of all things evil. Jesus described Satan—or the devil—and his human followers this way: "You belong to your father, the devil, and you want to carry out your father's desires. He was a murderer from the beginning, not holding to the truth, for there is no truth in him. When he lies, he speaks his native language, for he is a liar and the father of lies" (John 8:44).

What Does This Mean for You?

There is a war going on, but it is not a war you can see. It's spiritual warfare. Although God and the devil are in battle, you don't have to wait until the end to see who will win. God has already defeated Satan and the power of sin and death with Christ's sacrifice on the cross. When the time is right, God will cast Satan and his angels into "the lake of fire and brimstone," where they will remain for eternity (Revelation 20:10 NKJV).

Today and every day Satan is still trying to wreak as much havoc as possible. He is still using the same old schemes and tactics he has used on other people through the ages to tempt you to sin. The apostle John described our weaknesses as the lust of the flesh, the lust of the eyes, and the pride of life (1 John 2:16). Don't let Satan attack you through your weaknesses. Follow these three practices prescribed in the Bible:

> —"Put on the full armor of God, so that you can take your stand against the devil's schemes" (Ephesians 6:11).

> —"Be alert and of sober mind. Your enemy the devil prowls around like a roaring lion looking for someone to devour. Resist him, standing firm in the faith" (1 Peter 5:8-9).

> —"Submit yourselves, then, to God. Resist the devil, and he will flee from you" (James 4:7).

44

When God Makes a Promise, He Keeps It

*God is not human, that he should lie, not a human
being, that he should change his mind. Does he speak
and then not act? Does he promise and not fulfill?
(Numbers 23:19).*

*He is the Maker of heaven and earth, the sea, and
everything in them—he remains faithful forever
(Psalm 146:6).*

*God did this so that, by two unchangeable things in which
it is impossible for God to lie, we who have fled to take
hold of the hope set before us may be greatly encouraged
(Hebrews 6:18).*

What is a promise? The dictionary defines the word *promise* as "a statement, either oral or written, assuring that one will or will not do something." It's a vow or a pledge.

You've probably made a few vows and pledges in your lifetime, right? If you're married, you promised or vowed to love and honor your spouse until death. If you've been in the military, you made an oath to honor and serve. Even church members make pledges to God and the other church members of their desire to be part of a specific church fellowship. So just about everyone has some experience with promises, vows, and pledges. But in this chapter, we are not looking at *our* ability to keep a promise. Rather, we are looking at *God's* ability to keep His promises. We are learning about the truthfulness of God.

The Nature of God

Theologians call God's truthfulness "veracity." This word has its origin in medieval Latin and means "true." God, by His very nature, represents all things as they really are. God's veracity is evident in His promises, and in His ability to follow through and keep His promises.

This is important because *the power of a promise depends on the power of the one making the promise.* Anyone can make a promise— and everyone does. But does the one making the pledge have the ability or power or authority to fulfill it? When it comes to God, we can have full confidence that He can and will keep His promises.

The prophet Samuel said to Saul, "He who is the Glory of Israel [God] does not lie or change his mind; for he is not a human being, that he should change his mind" (1 Samuel 15:29). The apostle Paul also spoke of the nature of God as He "who does not lie" (Titus 1:2). In Hebrews 6:18, we read that "it is impossible for God to lie." As a result of God's truthfulness, "we who have fled to take hold of the hope set before us may be greatly encouraged."

Because God Himself is truth and the source of truth, it is impossible for Him to say anything untruthful. The passages above affirm not just that God does not lie, but that He cannot lie. Lying is completely contrary to His very nature.

Therefore, people can trust in God's promises as revealed in the Bible. If God said it, we can believe it!

The Nature of Promises in the Bible

Every promise God has made in the Bible will be fulfilled. But when you look at His promises, you have to ask yourself: To whom did God make this promise? It would be a mistake for you to assume that every promise made in the Bible has application to you today.

Many of God's promises were limited to specific people or groups of people. That means these promises apply to them. Other promises, though they were made in connection with a specific situation, do have a universal application for all time. These types of promises can apply to believers today, including you.

For example, consider the promise in 1 Kings 8:56. It is considered to be a specific promise but also has universal application: "Praise be to the LORD, who has given rest to his people Israel just as he promised. Not one word has failed of all the good promises he gave through his servant Moses." King Solomon, David's son, had just offered up a prayer of dedication to God for the newly completed temple in Jerusalem. In that prayer, Solomon recounted before the Lord all that he had done for His people, the Jews. After completing his prayer, Solomon turned around and made the statement in verse 56. He reminded the people of Israel that God had given them peace, just as He had promised. And he said that God always keeps His promises.

The people of Israel could count on God to keep His promises, and because God is consistent, we today can always count on Him to keep His promises.

The Nature of God's Promises to You

There is one more point to keep in mind about God's promises: Many of them are conditional. That is, God will promise to do or give something, but we are expected to do or give something as well. Consider this promise made to the nation of Israel: "If you fully obey the LORD your God and carefully follow all his commands I give you today, the LORD your God will set you high above all the nations on earth" (Deuteronomy 28:1). This is an "if-then" promise, a promise with a condition. Did you notice the word "if" at the beginning of the promise? *If* the people of Israel obeyed the Lord, *then* God would make His people greater than any other nation on Earth. God's promise was given with a condition.

What Does This Mean for You?

God does not casually make promises then never get around to fulfilling them. Every promise found in Scripture has a purpose, and every one will be kept. Some of God's promises are made to specific people, but there are many others that are offered to you today. These promises are in the Bible for the taking. God would not offer what He cannot do or is unwilling to do. So you can be 100 percent assured of the legitimacy of His promises.

When it comes to putting God's powerful promises to work in your life, the issue will never be about His trustworthiness or His ability to fulfill the promise. When it comes to the conditional promises, the fulfillment always depends on you. You must fulfill your part of the promise (the "if" part) and trust in God's ability to follow through and do His part (the "then" part). So check your obedience on the "if" factor when you look for God to fulfill a promise.

What, then, is required of you? In a word, *obedience.* An all-powerful God is offering you all-powerful promises. All He is asking from you is...

> —a willingness to follow Him even though at times you stumble and fall (Philippians 3:14),
>
> —a willingness to ask for forgiveness when you falter (1 John 1:9), and
>
> —a willingness to stay in the battle (and it is a battle!) of becoming a man or woman after God's own heart (Acts 13:22).

45

Jesus Walks with You, and When Necessary, Carries You

I know whom I have believed, and am convinced that he is able to guard what I have entrusted to him until that day (2 Timothy 1:12).

I write these things to you who believe in the name of the Son of God so that you may know that you have eternal life (1 John 5:13).

He tends his flock like a shepherd: He gathers the lambs in his arms and carries them close to his heart (Isaiah 40:11).

During the French and Indian War in North America, a group of American soldiers known as Rogers' Rangers fought for the British against the French. They used a combination of pioneer techniques and Native American tactics to outsmart enemy soldiers in wooded terrain where traditional militias struggled. These soldiers were also known for holding a certain standard: leave no fellow soldier behind.

The concept of leaving no one behind is also central to the Bible's teaching on the assurance of salvation. The issue is simple: Can a truly saved person ever lose his or her salvation and be "left behind"?

The biblical reality is that a truly saved person can have assurance that Jesus is always present with him and, when necessary, will carry him. We have the assurance that no matter what happens to us here on Earth, we will make it to heaven.

Assurance of salvation is based on the promise of God. God will not leave any of His children behind. In Genesis, He told Jacob, "I will not leave you until I have done what I have promised you" (Genesis 28:15). The New Testament repeats this promise when it states, "God has said, 'Never will I leave you; never will I forsake you'" (Hebrews 13:5). The God who cannot lie has promised we can have assurance of our salvation—that we will never be left behind!

Assurance of salvation is based on the work of God. If you are a believer, you can be confident "that he who began a good work in you will carry it on to completion until the day of Christ Jesus" (Philippians 1:6). Once God has made you alive in Christ and placed the Holy Spirit in you, the work of salvation will continue until you see Jesus face-to-face in heaven.

Assurance of salvation is based on the power of God. At times you may sin and wrongly feel as though your sin is too great for God to forgive, and therefore think that God has abandoned you. But the apostle Paul, who labeled himself "the worst" of sinners (1 Timothy 1:15), was assured that God's power was sufficient to save him:

> I am convinced that neither death nor life, neither angels nor demons, neither the present nor the future, nor any powers, neither height nor depth, nor anything else in all creation, will be able to separate us from the love of God that is in Christ Jesus our Lord (Romans 8:38-39).

Assurance of salvation is based on the resurrection of Christ. Followers of the risen Christ were turned into a courageous band of witnesses and martyrs who, in a few years, spread the gospel across the Roman Empire. Their belief in the resurrection could not be obliterated by ridicule, prison, torture, or even death. No fear or dread in this life could quench the hope and joy that came from the assurance of their salvation. Their faith was based on Jesus' promise, "I am the resurrection and the life. The one who believes in me will live, even though they die" (John 11:24).

Assurance of salvation is based on the indwelling Holy Spirit. Jesus said He would come to make His home in each believer (John 14:23), and that that relationship would be permanently sealed with the Holy Spirit (Ephesians 4:30). We find further affirmation of our relationship with God in Romans 8:15-16: "The Spirit you received brought about your adoption to sonship. And by him we cry, 'Abba, Father.' The Spirit himself testifies with our spirit that we are God's children" (Romans 8:15-16).

Assurance of salvation does not mean there are no doubts. Doubt happens when we take our eyes off God and fail to remember His assurances that He will be with us to the end of our lives and beyond.

Satan, "the accuser of our brothers and sisters" (Revelation 12:10), also does his part to cause Christians to doubt. Satan cannot affect our salvation, but he can make us doubt God by using the same tactics he used on Eve. He planted doubt in her mind by asking, "Did God really say...?" (Genesis 3:1).

Living with unresolved sin can also cause a believer to doubt their salvation. Their sin keeps them from enjoying an open relationship with God. They experience the physical and mental anguish King David went through after his sin with Bathsheba: "When I kept silent, my bones wasted away" (Psalm 32:3). Finally David said, "I will confess my transgressions to the LORD." And what happened? God "forgave the guilt of [his] sin" (verse 5). Christians cannot lose their salvation with unconfessed sin, but they can lose out on sweet fellowship with God.

Many Christians have doubts based on whether or not they have done enough good works. They wonder, *Have I done enough? Have I done my part? Or have I fallen short of what God expects of me?*

If that describes you, remember what Ephesians 2:8-9 says: "It is by grace you have been saved, through faith—and this is not from yourselves, it is the gift of God—not by works, so that no one can boast." Assurance is not based on *your* works, but on *Christ's* work on the cross on your behalf.

Finally, there are those who lack assurance of salvation because they lack a Savior. They have never really believed in Jesus as their Lord and Savior. They may have gone through the motions, like praying a prayer, walking an aisle, or raising a hand, but they still do not know salvation. This is the only legitimate reason to experience doubt over one's salvation. Doubt in this case is a good thing because it can lead to salvation when a person realizes his or her need to truly turn to God in full faith for the gift of salvation.

What Does This Mean for You?

Assurance is a trust issue. If you are putting your trust in your own abilities or in your religious works, you will never be assured of salvation. Why? Because your trust is in the wrong thing! Only Christ can offer and give you eternal life. Trusting in the God of the universe to save you will give you complete confidence and assurance. Personal assurance of salvation is a lot like going to the airport with a confirmed ticket to your destination. You can relax knowing that, with that ticket, you are assured of a seat on the plane bound for the destination of your choice.

If Jesus is your Savior, He has bought you a ticket to heaven. He paid for it with His death and resurrection.

It is reassuring to know that even if you are abandoned by family or friends, Jesus is always there for you and with you. He will comfort you, protect you, give you the strength you need, and if necessary, even carry you—not only through your trials, but to your eternal home in heaven.

46

This News Is So Good, Don't Keep It to Yourself!

What I received I passed on to you as of first importance: that Christ died for our sins according to the Scriptures, that he was buried, that he was raised on the third day according to the Scriptures (1 Corinthians 15:3–4).

Jesus said, "I am the resurrection and the life. The one who believes in me will live, even though they die" (John 11:25).

The Spirit of holiness was appointed the Son of God in power by his resurrection from the dead: Jesus Christ our Lord (Romans 1:4).

What's the greatest news you've ever received? And once you heard it, how hard was it to contain that news, to not rush to your phone or out into the streets and share it with anyone who would listen? Was it the fact that you were expecting your first child? Or you received that big promotion? Or you were informed by your doctor that you're finally cancer-free? All of these news items are noteworthy—and worthy of celebrating. But the greatest news ever came almost 2000 years ago when Jesus' disciples heard and saw that their friend, teacher, and leader was alive from the dead (Acts 4:33). Now that's incredible news!

Because of the visible proof of His resurrection, Jesus' broken-hearted followers turned into a courageous band of witnesses who, without threat of reprisal, retaliation, or even fear of death, took to the streets to tell anyone who would listen to the good news. What was the result of that excitement? In just a few years, their message had spread to the distant regions of the Roman Empire. How are you doing in this department? Are you as excited as the early disciples were about sharing the good news? Here are some important truths to keep in mind about the resurrection:

The resurrection is foundational to the Christian faith. The resurrection of Jesus is at the heart of the Christian faith. Jesus promised His resurrection, and the fact it really happened shows the world that Christ has power over death and is *the* ruler of God's eternal kingdom. Jesus was not a false prophet or impostor. Of all the religious leaders who have ever lived, only Jesus rose from the dead. Because of His bodily resurrection, those who have placed their faith in Him can be certain of their resurrection as well, as explained in Romans 6:4: "We were therefore buried with him through baptism into death in order that, just as Christ was raised from the dead through the glory of the Father, we too may live a new life."

The resurrection is the focal point of the Christian message. The first two sermons Peter preached after Christ's resurrection focused on the resurrection (see Acts 2:14-36; 3:12-26). Paul also made it clear the resurrection was a key element of Christianity. He said, "What I received I passed on to you as of first importance" (1 Corinthians 15:3). Paul then went on to list all those who had seen the resurrected Jesus:

> He appeared to Cephas, and then to the Twelve.
> After that, he appeared to more than five hundred
> of the brothers and sisters at the same time, most of
> whom are still living, though some have fallen asleep.

> Then he appeared to James, then to all the apostles,
> and last of all he appeared to me also, as to one abnor-
> mally born (1 Corinthians 15:5-8).

The resurrection is not a myth or a fantasy that was cooked up by a bunch of frightened fisherman who had lost their leader.

The resurrection is certain because of Christ's resurrection.

- —Because Christ rose, we know that what He promised is true—He is God.

- —Because Christ rose, we have assurance that our sins
  are forgiven.

- —Because Christ rose, He lives and sits at the right
  hand of the Father interceding for us.

- —Because Christ rose, He defeated death for us.

Therefore, we know we will also be raised.

The resurrection is our hope of eternal life. All religions speak of some sort of life after death. But it's all just talk. All other religions offer an uncertain kind of hope, a hope that has no proof. Only Christianity gives a certain hope that death has been conquered. Why? Because Jesus was raised from the dead. Again, no other religion offers a leader who has risen from the dead. Jesus' own resurrection is proof that those who believe in Him will also be raised from the dead to live in new bodies for all eternity with Jesus. This was Jesus' promise: "If I go and prepare a place for you, I will come back and take you to be with me that you also may be where I am" (John 14:3).

The resurrection includes both body and soul. Paul wrote to a church in the city of Corinth, which was situated in the heart of Greek culture. According to Greek philosophers, the soul was the real person, imprisoned in a physical body, and at death, the soul was released. Christianity, by contrast, teaches that the body and soul will be united in the resurrection. As Paul explained to the Corinthians,

"So will it be with the resurrection of the dead. The body that is sown is perishable, it is raised imperishable" (1 Corinthians 15:42).

Your resurrected body will be eternal. Do you like what you look like? Well, get used to it, because your resurrected body will have a similar appearance but be different in substance. After the resurrection, when Jesus miraculously appeared to His disciples through closed doors, they recognized Him—"the disciples were overjoyed when they saw the Lord" (John 20:20). Your resurrected body will be better than you can imagine. You will still have your own personality and distinctives, but these will be perfected through Christ's work. There will be no more sickness and death. You will live forever!

What Does This Mean for You?

The fact of the resurrection should give you a sure hope about the future and make you more excited about your faith. Christ's resurrection is proof that death is no longer to be feared. Whether you die next week, next month, or many years later in the future, it doesn't matter. Why? Because you have no reason to fear death. You understand what Jesus was saying to His disciples, and now to you: "I am the resurrection and the life. The one who believes in me will live, even though they die" (John 11:25).

You might be thinking, *If I had been there and witnessed Jesus alive from the dead, I could be as excited as those early disciples.* But you were not there. You are alive on Earth these 2000 years later. Should that make any difference? No, and Peter didn't think so either when he wrote: "Though now you do not see Him, yet believing, you rejoice with joy inexpressible and full of glory, receiving the end of your faith—the salvation of your souls" (1 Peter 1:8-9 NKJV).

Peter said you should be rejoicing with joy inexpressible. Your joy should be so visible that people around you can't help but notice something different about you. Is that joy visible? If not, maybe it's time for you to refresh your understanding of the implications of the resurrection on your life. Then, with renewed excitement, remember: This news is so good you don't want to keep it to yourself!

47

You Ain't Seen Nothing Yet!

Blessed are you when people insult you, persecute you and falsely say all kinds of evil against you because of me. Rejoice and be glad, because great is your reward in heaven (Matthew 5:11-12).

I saw "a new heaven and a new earth," for the first heaven and the first earth had passed away, and there was no longer any sea. I saw the Holy City, the new Jerusalem, coming down out of heaven from God, prepared as a bride beautifully dressed for her husband. And I heard a loud voice from the throne saying, "Look! God's dwelling place is now among the people, and he will dwell with them. They will be his people, and God himself will be with them and be their God. He will wipe every tear from their eyes. There will be no more death or mourning or crying or pain, for the old order of things has passed away" (Revelation 21:1-4).

While I was doing research about hell for another of the 50 teachings in this book, I noticed that the topic that preceded *hell* was the topic *heaven*. I thought to myself: *How appropriate that these two vital topics would be back-to-back in my reference book.*

It is appropriate because heaven and hell are "bookends" for what God has done, is doing, and will do in the future. Hell is a real place created before time for the devil and his angels (Matthew 25:41). To find out what the Bible has to say about hell, read chapter 39, "Turn or Burn." But right now we are looking at the opposite of hell—heaven, about which we could say, "You ain't seen nothing yet!"

As we begin looking at what the Bible teaches about heaven, we first need to know that in Scripture, the word *heaven* can refer most generally to one of three realms—to the atmospheric space immediately above us, to the celestial heaven that includes the universe, or to the abode of God.

The Atmospheric Heavens

The atmospheric heavens include the space that immediately surrounds the Earth, the air that we breathe, which extends up about 20 miles. The most frequently occurring atmospheric phenomenon in Scripture is rain, and on rare occasions, snow. Isaiah 55:9-10 speaks of this realm when it says, "As the heavens are higher than the earth, so are my ways higher than your ways and my thoughts than your thoughts. As the rain and the snow come down from heaven…"

The Celestial Heavens

If you've ever taken a tour of an observatory, you may have heard the tour guide refer to the great expanse of the universe as heaven. And that's exactly what God called His work at the time of creation. God said, "Let there be lights in the firmament of the heavens to divide the day from the night; and let them be for signs and seasons, and for days and years" (Genesis 1:14 NKJV). The writer of the book of Hebrews stated, "The heavens are the work of your hands" (Hebrews 1:10). And in Job 9:9, God is said to be the "Maker of the Bear and Orion, the Pleiades and the constellations of the south."

Heaven as the Abode of God

It is true the Bible teaches that "the heavens, even the highest heaven, cannot contain [God]" (1 Kings 8:27), and that God is everywhere present in the universe. But at the same time, the Bible also clearly states that heaven is the habitation of God: "I live in a high and holy place" (Isaiah 57:15). In multiple Old Testament passages God is given the title "the God of heaven" (for example, Nehemiah 1:4-5).

The Present Inhabitants of Heaven

Not only does the Father dwell in heaven, Jesus does too. He sits at the Father's right hand, according to Acts 5:31: "God exalted him to his own right hand as Prince and Savior." It is from there that Jesus intercedes for believers (Romans 8:34).

Heaven is also the abode of the good angels. At the birth of Jesus, they were described as the "heavenly host" (Luke 2:13). They are presently "standing around the throne" (Revelation 7:11), and they "stand before God" (8:2).

The Future Inhabitants of Heaven

Before Jesus left His disciples, He told them that He was returning to heaven to prepare a place for those who believe in Him. Jesus said, "My Father's house has many rooms; if that were not so, would I have told you that I am going there to prepare a place for you? And if I go and prepare a place for you, I will come back and take you to be with me that you also may be where I am" (John 14:2-3).

How is Jesus' return for His own described? "The Lord himself will come down from heaven, with a loud command, with the voice of the archangel and with the trumpet call of God, and the dead in Christ will rise first. After that, we who are still alive and are left will be caught up together with them in the clouds to meet the Lord in the air. And so we will be with the Lord forever" (1 Thessalonians 4:16-18).

A Description of Heaven

One way to gain a better understanding about a person is by seeing where they live. But with God, it's just the opposite! God is not a reflection of heaven. Rather, heaven is a reflection of the God who dwells there. The prophet Ezekiel recorded this vision of God in heaven:

> Spread out above the heads of the living creatures was what looked something like a vault, sparkling like crystal, and awesome... Then there came a voice from above the vault... Above the vault over their heads was what looked like a throne of lapis lazuli, and high above on the throne was a figure like that of a man. I saw that from what appeared to be his waist up he looked like glowing metal, as if full of fire, and that from there down he looked like fire; and brilliant light surrounded him. Like the appearance of a rainbow in the clouds on a rainy day, so was the radiance around him. This was the appearance of the likeness of the glory of the LORD. When I saw it, I fell facedown (Ezekiel 1:22-28).

Beginning with this picture of God and His heaven, imagine heaven as a place...

—with no sorrow, pain, or death (Revelation 21:4).

—with no more curse (21:4).

—with the glory of God as the only light needed (21:23).

—with a population of only those whose names are written in the Lamb's Book of Life (21:27).

—where God is worshipped and served day and night for eternity (7:15).

What Does This Mean for You?

Think of the most beautiful, elegant home, mansion, or palace you have ever visited. Do you have trouble trying to describe this place to others? Well, that's what you are faced with in trying to describe heaven. After all, it's the place where the God of the universe dwells. It's got to be impressive! But it isn't just the *place,* as beautiful as it may sound and is described in the Bible. It's the *person* that should draw you toward heaven—Jesus, the Lamb of God, your Savior.

While you are waiting to be welcomed to heaven, enjoy reading the scriptures that describe your future eternal home. Take time to be in awe of its indescribable glory. Look forward to being united with the Father and the Son in a place where "there will be no more death or mourning or crying or pain, for the old order of things has passed away" (Revelation 21:4)—a place of constant and perfect worship.

48

Nothing Takes God by Surprise

*Knowing their thoughts, Jesus said, "Why do you
entertain evil thoughts in your hearts?"
(Matthew 9:4).*

*Who knows a person's thoughts except their own
spirit within them? In the same way no one knows
the thoughts of God except the Spirit of God
(1 Corinthians 2:11).*

*Judge nothing before the appointed time; wait until
the Lord comes. He will bring to light what is hidden
in darkness and will expose the motives of the heart
(1 Corinthians 4:5).*

One of the by-products of a long-lasting marriage is the ability to anticipate what the other person is thinking. Often even before that partner opens their mouth, the other partner starts or completes what the other is about to say. People who live together for years are almost able, it seems, to read each other's minds and anticipate each other's actions. Pretty amazing, right?

However that is just the tip of the iceberg when compared to what God is able to do. God, as the Creator of all things, is also the possessor of all knowledge. He has all knowledge, and as Creator, He has created all knowledge. Theologians have labeled this attribute of God His *omniscience*. God has infinite knowledge of all things past, present, and future. In simple terms, *nothing takes God by surprise*.

Two aspects of God's infinite knowledge are emphasized in the Scriptures.

First, nothing happens anywhere or at any time of which He is ignorant. Man cannot hide either his actions or his thoughts from God. King David acknowledged this in Psalm 139:1-6:

> Verse 1—David said God's knowledge of him came as if He had combed through every detail of David's life and, as a result, knew David intimately: "You have searched me, LORD, and you know me."

> Verses 2-3—The Lord knew every move and action David made: "You know when I sit and when I rise; you perceive my thoughts from afar. You discern my going out and my lying down; you are familiar with all my ways." That God knew David's thoughts means He knew David's motivations. And not only did He perceive David's thoughts, but He did so "from afar."

> Verse 4—The Lord also knew what David would say before he spoke: "Before a word is on my tongue you, LORD, know it completely."

> Verse 5—The Lord had David surrounded with His knowledge and presence: "You hem me in behind and before, and you lay your hand upon me."

> Verse 6—David, in utter amazement at God's abilities, concluded his revelation by saying, "Such knowledge is too wonderful for me, too lofty for me to attain." In other words, divine omniscience is too lofty for humans to comprehend.

Not only did God know David well, but He knows the hearts of all people: "I am he who searches hearts and minds, and I will repay each of you according to your deeds" (Revelation 2:23).

Jesus, the Son of God, exhibited omniscience as well. In Matthew 9:4 we read, "Jesus said, 'Why do you entertain evil thoughts in your hearts?'" And later, in the book of Revelation, the Lord clearly described not only people's actions, but also their inner spiritual condition. With regard to the seven churches in Revelation chapters 2 and 3, the Lord said, "I know your deeds" (Revelation 2:1–3:22).

Throughout the Bible, we are repeatedly reminded that nothing happens anywhere without God's full knowledge.

Second, God is all-wise in His plans and purposes. God knows all things from the beginning, and He has plans for all things from the beginning.

God has a plan for the nation of Israel—In the Old Testament, God told the Israelites—through the prophet Jeremiah—that He had plans for them. The rebellious nation had been taken away captive into far-off Babylon. It looked like Israel was finished as a nation. But Jeremiah, speaking for God, told these displaced Jews that they would have a future. God said, "I know the plans I have for you…plans to prosper you and not to harm you, plans to give you hope and a future" (Jeremiah 29:11).

God promised Abraham that a great nation would come from his descendants. Even though the people of Israel had rebelled against God and were scattered to the far corners of the Earth, their future was still secure because of God's all-wise plan for bringing about the people's restoration and their participation in the Messiah's thousand-year reign on Earth.

God has a plan for His church—This plan for the church is not new. In fact, it's a plan from all eternity! The apostle Paul said it this way: "He chose us in Him before the foundation of the world, that we should be holy and without blame before Him in love" (Ephesians 1:4).

The New Testament is filled with details about God's plans and purposes for His church:

With all wisdom and understanding, he made known to us the mystery of his will according to his good pleasure, which he purposed in Christ, to be put into effect when the times reach their fulfillment—to bring unity to all things in heaven and on earth under Christ (Ephesians 1:8-10).

We know that in all things God works for the good of those who love him, who have been called according to his purpose. For those God foreknew he also predestined to be conformed to the image of his Son, that he might be the firstborn among many brothers and sisters (Romans 8:28-29).

What Does This Mean for You?

God's omniscience could be a problem for you if you are trying to hide some part of your life from Him. Some people prefer to deny that God is able to know their thoughts and actions, for they think that means they can go on with life without any concern for whether God will hold them accountable. Francis Thompson, in a poem, called God "the Hound of Heaven" because His omniscience will "hound" a person until he acknowledges God's control over his life. The fact that God is omniscient should serve as a restraining force in your life. You cannot hide anything from Him!

If you are a Christian, you won't be bothered by God's omniscience. In fact, the realization that God knows all things should give you great comfort and confidence. When you are tempted to doubt God or question His management of your life, or when circumstances look bleak, remember that God has a plan, and in the end, things will turn out for your good and His glory. You just need to have faith and trust that God knows what He is doing—because He does!

And here's another comforting thought: God will never forget about the day you asked Him to save your soul. Your name is written and preserved in the Lamb's Book of Life (Revelation 13:8). God knows you by name, and He never forgets the name of one of His children.

49

Heavenly Living Starts Here and Now

Praise be to the God and Father of our Lord Jesus
Christ, who has blessed us in the heavenly realms
with every spiritual blessing in Christ
(Ephesians 1:3).

Our citizenship is in heaven. And we eagerly await
a Savior from there, the Lord Jesus Christ, who, by
the power that enables him to bring everything
under his control, will transform our lowly bodies
so that they will be like his glorious body
(Philippians 3:20–21).

Did you know that all of what are called "the epistles" in the New Testament are actually letters written to individuals and churches to encourage, admonish, or at times rebuke the actions and attitudes of the readers? God not only superintended the writing of those letters for the benefit of the readers 2000 years ago, but He was writing those same letters for believers today! The things our fellow believers struggled with in the past are the same things we struggle with today. We too are having trouble conforming to the teachings of Christ.

Two of those letters were written to a church group in the Greek city of Corinth. The Christians there were a rowdy lot of believers who found it difficult to resist the negative influences of their pagan culture and their sin natures. The apostle Paul wrote to challenge them to "heavenly living."

> You are still worldly. For since there is jealousy and quarreling among you, are you not worldly? Are you not acting like mere humans? (1 Corinthians 3:3).

Paul admonished the people in the church at Corinth to act like heavenly citizens. When a person comes to Christ, he immediately becomes a citizen of heaven, and God expects him to assume a heavenly lifestyle. Since this is what is expected of every Christian, let's note what heavenly living will produce in our lives.

Heavenly living offers a different perspective. Because our citizenship is now in heaven, our involvement in this world—with its materialism and many godless activities—should cause us to live with discernment. Rather than seeking fulfillment from worldly pleasures, we should look for fulfillment from God and His Word, and through our associations with God's people.

Our focus should not be on "the horizontal" (our relationship with mankind and the world), but on "the vertical" (our relationship with God). We should keep our focus heavenward. In Colossians 3:1-2, Paul said, "Since, then, you have been raised with Christ, set your hearts on things above, where Christ is, seated at the right hand of God. Set your mind on things above, not on earthly things." That's what it means to focus on the vertical.

Heavenly living accomplishes the will of God. In the Lord's Prayer, Jesus taught us to say, "Your will be done, on earth as it is in heaven" (Matthew 6:10). God's will is for all Christians to be conformed to the image of His Son, the Lord Jesus (Romans 8:29). Therefore, heavenly living is synonymous with becoming more like Jesus.

How is this accomplished? As you are faithfully obedient to God's Word, you will live a Christ-honoring life, which is exactly what God desires of His people as citizens of heaven. The desire of every believer should be that whatever they do, they "do it all for the glory of God" (1 Corinthians 10:31).

Heavenly living gives priority to godly living. Letting heaven fill our thoughts means striving to put heaven's priorities into daily practice and concentrating on what is eternal rather than on what is temporal: "Whatever is true, whatever is noble, whatever is right, whatever is pure, whatever is lovely, whatever is admirable—if anything is excellent or praiseworthy—think about such things" (Philippians 4:8). And to make sure we have the power to keep our priorities straight, God has given us His Spirit and commands us to be obedient to the Spirit's prompting: "Walk by the Spirit, and you will not gratify the desires of the flesh" (Galatians 5:16).

Heavenly living will produce conflicts. Contrary to what some Christians think, God never promised believers a carefree life. In fact, Jesus said the more a believer identifies with Him, the more problems he will have. Jesus warned His followers about what heavenly living would produce: "Remember what I told you: 'A servant is not greater than his master.' If they persecuted me, they will persecute you also" (John 15:20).

And the battle does not end with personal conflicts. Besides being persecuted because we identify with Christ, we will also face opposition from the forces of evil. "Our struggle is not against flesh and blood, but against the rulers, against the authorities, against the powers of this dark world and against the spiritual forces of evil in the heavenly realms" (Ephesians 6:12). We can praise God, however, because we have victory over both evil men and evil forces "through our Lord Jesus Christ" (1 Corinthians 15:57).

Heavenly living produces future rewards. One reward believers experience as a result of heavenly living is immediate: They know they are honoring the Lord and serving His people. That would be blessing enough, but the Bible also teaches that what believers do for God here in this life will also result in further rewards in heaven. Paul affirmed this dual blessing when he wrote, "Godliness has value for all things, holding promise for both the present life and the life to come" (1 Timothy 4:8).

So as Christians, we should take heart. Even though we suffer, are often mistreated, and seem to receive few rewards for our faithfulness here on Earth, these things will pale in comparison to what Jesus has waiting for us in heaven. Jesus says, "Rejoice and be glad, because great is your reward in heaven, for in the same way they persecuted the prophets who were before you" (Matthew 5:12).

Heavenly living gives glory to God. What will believers be doing for all eternity? The Bible says we will be worshipping around the throne of God in heaven. We will be giving Him the honor He deserves. Isn't that how it should be after all He has done for us? Addressing the Corinthians, Paul wrote, "You were bought at a price." He then admonished his readers to "therefore honor God with your bodies" (1 Corinthians 6:20). That's what we will be doing in heaven for all eternity, and we can and should start doing that here on Earth.

What is to be our focus as we go through each day? "Whether you eat or drink or whatever you do, do it all for the glory of God" (1 Corinthians 10:31).

What Does This Mean for You?

When you trusted in Christ for salvation, you spiritually participated with the Lord in His crucifixion and His victory over sin and death (Galatians 2:20). Your "old self" is dead (Romans 6:6). As a new person, you have the indwelling Holy Spirit to empower you to live a godly life. He gives you the resources for heavenly living on Earth. With His help, you can do it! Paul told the Corinthians they had no excuse for their worldly behavior, and that goes for you too. Purpose and pray not to act like a mere human, but like the heavenly citizen you are.

50

In the End, God Wins!

The Lord himself will come down from heaven, with a loud command, with the voice of the archangel and with the trumpet call of God, and the dead in Christ will rise first. After that, we who are still alive and are left will be caught up together with them in the clouds to meet the Lord in the air. And so we will be with the Lord forever (1 Thessalonians 4:16–17).

Then the end will come, when he hands over the kingdom to God the Father after he has destroyed all dominion, authority and power. For he must reign until he has put all his enemies under his feet. The last enemy to be destroyed is death (1 Corinthians 15:24–26).

Recently I finished a story that was the second in a series of three novels. I was looking forward to the last book, but the author made a critical error: He told me what was going to happen in the next book to my two favorite characters. They had, in a way, become my "friends," and I was being told they wouldn't be in the final book. Well, that did it for me. I never read the last book. I didn't want to face what was going to happen!

But that doesn't happen when I read about the future in my

Bible. Instead, I get excited. Why? Because in the end, God wins! This is good news in light of what we see happening around us today. Do you see much hope for mankind and our world? Evil is rampant, and it is only going to get worse. But things won't stay that way. The Bible says there is coming a day when God will destroy all evil and restore righteousness, and we who are Christians are on the winning team.

The Road to the Future

According to the Bible, there is a progression of future events that must take place in preparation for the complete and final manifestation of the kingdom of God. Theologians refer to this study of future things as *eschatology*.

Physical death—At physical death, the material aspect of your being, the body, will be separated from the immaterial aspect, the spirit. At this time, an intermediate state exists for both the righteous and the wicked after they die. The spirits of the righteous go to be with God (Philippians 1:21-23) while their physical bodies stay on Earth. The spirits of the wicked dead go to hades (Luke 16:23) to await the final judgment and the second death, the lake of fire (Revelation 20:14-15) while their physical bodies also stay on Earth.

The second coming—This event will have two stages. In the first stage, Christ returns to Earth for His followers, both dead and alive, and takes them back to heaven as He promised, where they will live with Him for eternity (1 Thessalonians 4:16-17). His coming is "in the air" and will only affect believers. This stage is called the *rapture*, a term that comes from the phrase "caught up" (1 Thessalonians 4:17). In that moment believers will have their corrupted earthly bodies reunited with their spirits as new resurrected bodies. This event will happen in the "twinkling of an eye" (1 Corinthians 15:52).

In the second stage of Jesus' return, He is "coming with the clouds" and "every eye will see Him, even those who pierced him" (Revelation 1:7). He is coming as the Messiah and will establish

His earthly kingdom in Jerusalem and rule over the nations for 1000 years.

The resurrection of the dead—This too will be twofold.

> The resurrection of the just—This will occur at the time of the rapture. The dead in Christ as well as those who are still alive will experience a literal, bodily resurrection (1 Corinthians 15:22).

> The resurrection of the unjust—will come after the 1000-year reign of Christ and right before the final judgment (Revelation 20:7-15).

The judgments—As early as Genesis 2:17 God said, "You will certainly die" (Genesis 2:17) referring to judgment. Judgment day will come, and no one can escape it. More specifically, the Bible describes a series of judgments:

> The judgment of believers—This is not actually a judgment, because believers' sins were judged at the cross. "There is now no condemnation for those who are in Christ Jesus" (Romans 8:1). This event will be like the judging at a county fair, where rewards are distributed to successful contestants. "At that time each will receive their praise from God" (1 Corinthians 4:5). We could also call this judgment an awards ceremony.

> The judgment of Israel—This will be for the children of Israel and will occur at the beginning of the millennium, or the 1000-year reign of the Messiah, Jesus Christ. This judgment will be in preparation for the Jewish people to live and rule with their Messiah in the Davidic kingdom (Matthew 19:28; Luke 22:30).

> The judgment of the living nations—This will occur at the beginning of the millennium. It will take place on Earth in the "Valley of Jehoshaphat," possibly near Jerusalem. Jesus will judge the nations "for what they

did to my inheritance, my people Israel, because they scattered my people among the nations and divided up my land" (Joel 3:2).

The judgment of fallen angels—This will take place during the period known as "the great Day" (Jude 6). Satan will have his final judgment just preceding the final judgment of the wicked. The Bible doesn't say it specifically, but we can conclude that all fallen angels will be judged at this time (Revelation 20:10).

The judgment at the Great White Throne—This will be the final judgment of the wicked, which will forever settle their destiny of doom. The judge will be God, the Son. The standard will be perfection. This judgment will be based upon the things recorded in "the books" (Revelation 20:12). In case something might have been overlooked, there is a final appeal made to "the book of life" to see if their names are written in it. Only believers in Christ have their names written in this book.

The new heaven and new earth—God will make these new abodes after the 1000-year reign of Christ and the Great White Throne Judgment. All things will be returned to the way they were designed by God. In sinless glory, He will create a new heaven and a new earth. "Now I saw a new heaven and a new earth, for the first heaven and the first earth had passed away...the holy city, New Jerusalem, coming down out of heaven from God, prepared as a bride adorned for her husband" (Revelation 21:1-2).

What Does This Mean for You?

The Bible contains the complete story of the world from beginning to end, starting in Genesis and concluding in Revelation. There is no guesswork needed with regard to who created time and put the world in motion, and who will establish a new creation in the end. It is God, and He wants you to know your past and your future. In the past, God sent His Son to die for your sins. If you have acknowledged Christ's payment for your sins, that salvation will be realized with the return of Jesus Christ and you will live with Him forever in heaven.

With the knowledge that your past is taken care of and your future is secure, you now can focus on the present. Pray daily for the Holy Spirit to empower you to walk by the Spirit and live for Christ. Anchor your faith in the Word of God. Remain spiritually alert as you await the return of Christ. While the battle isn't over yet, the victory is assured!

Other Books by Jim George

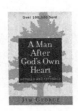

A Man After God's Own Heart

Many Christian men want to be men after God's own heart...but how do they do this? George shows that a heartfelt desire to practice God's priorities is all that's needed. God's grace does the rest.

A Man After God's Own Heart Devotional

This book is filled with quick, focused devotions that will encourage your spiritual growth, equip you to persevere when life gets tough, manage your responsibilities well with wisdom, and live with maximum impact in all you do.

A Husband After God's Own Heart

You'll find your marriage growing richer and deeper as you pursue God and discover 12 areas in which you can make a real difference in your relationship with your wife.

A Leader After God's Own Heart

Every man is either a leader or a leader in the making—whether at work, in the home, or any other setting. So what does it take to be a good leader—one God can use? This book will equip you to lead with strength and have a positive, lasting impact.

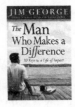

The Man Who Makes a Difference

How can you have a lasting impact? Here are the secrets to having a positive and meaningful influence in the lives of everyone you meet, including your wife and children.

A Young Man After God's Own Heart

Pursuing God really *is* an adventure—a lot like climbing a mountain. There are many challenges on the way up, but the great view at the top is well worth the trip. This book helps young men to experience the thrill of knowing real success in life—the kind that counts with God.

A Young Man's Guide to Discovering His Bible

God's Word can change your life—for real. But that can't happen until you commit yourself to knowing the Bible. That's what this book by bestselling author Jim George is all about—knowing your Bible, discovering what it says, and making it your personal guide. You'll be surprised how relevant the Bible is in everything you do!

A Young Man's Guide to Making Right Choices

This book will help teen guys to think carefully about their decisions, assuring they gain the skills needed to face life's challenges.

Bare Bones Bible® Handbook

The perfect resource for a fast and friendly overview of every book of the Bible. Excellent for anyone who wants to know the Bible better and get more from their interaction with God's Word.

The Bare Bones Bible® Handbook for Teens

Based on the bestselling *Bare Bones Bible® Handbook*, this edition includes content and life applications specially written with teens in mind. They will be amazed at how much the Bible has to say about the things that matter most to them.

10 Minutes to Knowing the Men and Women of the Bible

The lessons you can learn from the outstanding men and women of the Bible are powerfully relevant for today. As you review their lives, you'll discover special qualities worth emulating and life lessons for everyday living.

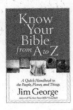

Know Your Bible from A to Z

This is a concise, easy-to-understand A-to-Z survey of the Bible's most important people, places, customs, and events. A great help for understanding the big picture of the Bible and applying the Scriptures to your daily life.

A Couple After God's Own Heart

Jim and Elizabeth George

Experience the excitement and love God always intended, and enjoy a relationship that reflects the love of Christ. Whether you're taking the first steps on your marriage journey or you've been on the road for years, you'll be refreshed and renewed by this book.

A Couple After God's Own Heart Interactive Workbook

Jim and Elizabeth George

Designed to work together with Jim and Elizabeth George's book *A Couple After God's Own Heart*, this interactive workbook will enable you and your spouse to experience more of the incredible bliss only God can bring into a marriage!

A Boy After God's Own Heart

This book helps boys learn how to make good decisions and great friends, see the benefits of homework and chores, get along better with their parents and siblings, and get into the Bible and grow closer to God.

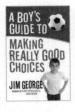

A Boy's Guide to Making Really Good Choices

Making good choices is the biggest step a boy can take toward growing up. This book helps boys learn to make the best kinds of choices—those that make them stronger, wiser, and more mature.

God's Wisdom for Little Boys

(coauthored with Elizabeth George)

The wonderful teachings of Proverbs come to life for boys. Memorable rhymes play alongside colorful paintings for a charming presentation of truths to live by.

About the Author

Jim George is the bestselling author of *The Bare Bones Bible® Handbook* and *A Man After God's Own Heart*, and has a total of more than 1 million books in print. He is a popular speaker at Christian events.

For further information about Jim's speaking ministry, visit his website:

www.JimGeorge.com

To learn more about Harvest House books and
to read sample chapters, visit our website:

www.harvesthousepublishers.com

HARVEST HOUSE PUBLISHERS
EUGENE, OREGON